TURNING LEAD INTO GOLD

TURNING LEAD INTO GOLD

The Transformative Alchemy of Waldorf Teaching

Jack Petrash

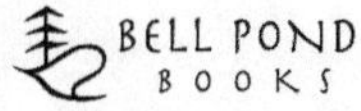
BELL POND
BOOKS

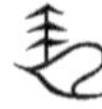

BELL POND BOOKS

An imprint of SteinerBooks / Anthroposophic Press, Inc.
PO Box 58 | Hudson, NY 12534
www.steinerbooks.org

Design by Jens Jensen
Cover by Angelica Hesse
(yellowpantsstudio.com)

LIBRARY OF CONGRESS CONTROL NUMBER: 2022941217
ISBN: 978-1-952166-11-2 (paperback)

Printed in the United States of America

Contents

For Carol

Who knows all of my lead,
but still chooses to see the gold.

Last night as I lay sleeping,
I dreamt that I had a beehive
here inside my heart.
And the golden bees
were making white combs
and sweet honey
from my old failures.

ANTONIO MACHADO

INTRODUCTION

We started out walking. It was early September, the year after I graduated my fourth eighth-grade class. My wife Carol and I were on the Camino de Santiago. Walking in September seemed perfect, because at that time of the year part of me would feel misplaced if I wasn't teaching. If it was September, I was supposed to be at school preparing my classroom, lettering name tags, and setting out supplies. But we had "retired" and this allowed us to do something we had considered for several years. We were walking the 500-mile pilgrimage across northern Spain. It turned out to be a journey through time.

Simply hiking ten miles each day with a back pack for eight weeks under sunny skies took us through a delightful harvest of grapes, figs, almonds, and chestnuts. But there was much more that was harvested along the way. Although walking is a physical activity, quite strenuous at times while traversing four mountain ranges with their continual *arriba* and *abajo*, there were so many surprising thoughts that rose in my mind—teaching memories, memories of colleagues and former students, and, of course, the parents. These memories surfaced unexpectedly, and not all of them were comforting. In many instances these recollections brought with them a new perspective and an understanding of past events that surprised me, allowed my defenses to drop, and caused my awareness to shift and deepen. The Camino was in so many ways a life review, a transformative experience just like teaching.

I needed to teach four classes from grade one to eight, because I require a considerable amount of time to learn. The ancient Greeks had two words for time: *Chronos* and *Kairos*. *Chronos* is chronological time, and my Waldorf class teaching began in the early seventies and ended in 2015; it all took place at the Washington Waldorf School. *Kairos*, on the other hand, is different. Richard Rohr, the writer and Franciscan priest, calls *Kairos* "deep time." Deep time is set apart from the normal calendar of events. The birth of a child, our wedding, the death of a loved one are days that exist singularly and have their own unique time. This is true, as well, when we experience moments of true understanding—what we might call epiphanies. My teaching journey had its epiphanies.

The pieces in this book come mostly from moments in deep time, moments when I found myself thinking somewhat shamefacedly, "Oh, now I get it." And, interestingly enough, a good many of those moments of insight occurred with classroom experiences when I clearly "didn't get it," moments when my teaching was misguided and flawed. I have heard that in anthroposophical medicine "pain can be seen as a substitute for consciousness." In that spirit I have thankfully found that my painful teaching experiences raised my conscious awareness of how I needed to work with students. This is the transformative alchemy of my Waldorf teaching journey, and it is at the heart of this book, *Turning Lead into Gold*.

Some of the chapters have previously been published. Others grew out of the work that I did training teachers through the Nova Institute and at the Rudolf Steiner Institute. My work with teachers made it necessary for me to continually reread Rudolf Steiner's basic books and essential educational lectures. Henry David Thoreau said that, if you want to see something new, walk the path you walked yesterday. This was the case with my rereading of Steiner, which helped to deepen my understanding of Waldorf education and to develop anthroposophical and pedagogical habits of mind, understandings that I brought with me into the classroom each day. These habits of mind matured over time and eventually gave rise to moments of fresh insight for my teaching.

I don't really know what kind of teacher I would have been without those new understandings. I do know that I continued to make mistakes; hopefully, they were smaller. But most important, the transformation of some of those mistakes into something golden would not have happened without the alchemy of Waldorf education and ever-present help of the spiritual world.

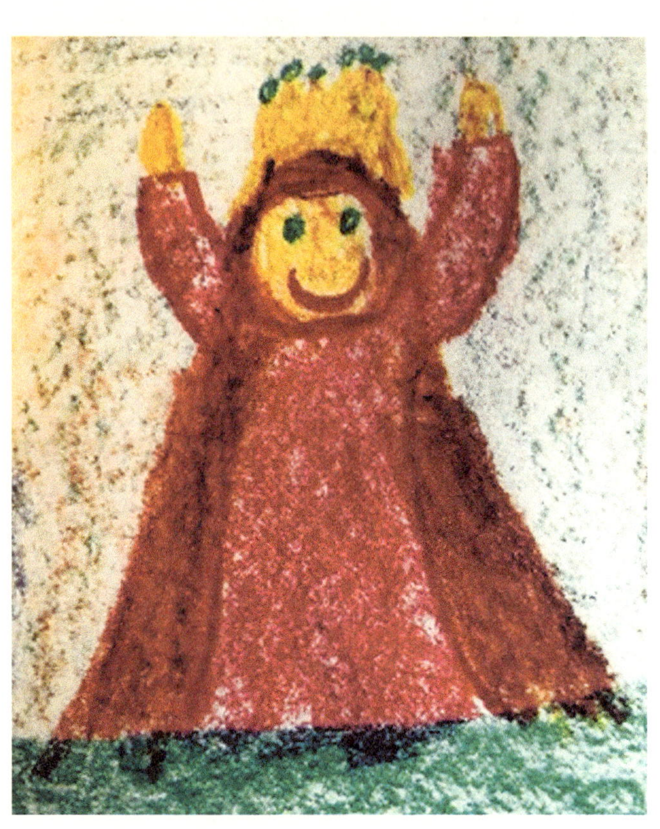

Part One

The Early Grades

I

What Made Me Think I Could Do This?

What made me think I could still teach? That's the question I am asking myself as I stand in front of a group of first graders a month into the school year. I am beset with doubts. I made the unexpected decision to teach a fourth class at the Washington Waldorf School, where I had previously taken three classes from grades one to eight. I made the decision for good reasons. After seven years of directing a small non-profit full-time and consulting with schools, I felt that I needed to be learning more about teaching, and what better way to do that than by working with children. But they say, "Be careful what you wish for." Well, I was clearly getting to see what that means.

First grade students put no stock in your reputation. Forget the terms "experienced teacher," "master teacher," whatever. These students hardly listened to me. They spoke out whenever they felt like it. Some of them threw tantrums. One or two even crawled under their desks when they didn't like what they were being asked to do. I was stunned. I had taught three classes from first grade to eighth, my first class when I was only twenty-four years old, and it had never been like this. If I hadn't felt so completely ashamed, I might have gone to the faculty and said, "I think I've made a mistake." I had hit a wall, a twenty-four-student wall, but I shouldn't have been surprised. I had been warned.

When I was introduced to the parents of this new class in the spring, prior to first grade, each parent was asked to say a little bit about their child and why they chose our school. Repeatedly I heard the phrase, "I have a strong child." I knew this was code for something. Now I was finding out what the phrase really meant.

I am also no stranger to the late summer "teacher nightmare," the one many of us get a week or two before school starts. This time I was standing in the first-grade room with my new students, and they were all out of their seats, clustered in the middle of the room. I asked the children to sit down, but there was no response. I repeated my request several times—nothing. I was bewildered, and that was how the school year started.

I must admit that throughout my years of teaching, my "low points" have always helped me to become a better teacher. My reflex, when I hit bottom, is to go back to the source, to the inner work that helps reorient and redirect me. So, when this occurred with the first grade, I picked up a book that had been sitting on my bookshelf gathering dust, *Rudolf Steiner in the Waldorf School*. I had purchased this book on the recommendation of an accomplished teacher from another Waldorf school, Roberto Trostli. We were standing together at a book table at a conference in Spring Valley, and he asked if I had read this book. When I told him no, he said that I should buy the book and that I would like it. So, I did, but it sat unopened on my bookshelf for years.

I believe that timing is everything, particularly with books. It was that way with *The Count of Monte Cristo*, which I bought in college but only read—and loved—ten years later when I was teaching seventh grade. And it was true for Mary

Fullerson's book, *By a New and Living Way,* which I lost for six or so years and then found at the perfect time. That's what happened again. I opened the book that had been recommended and began reading an address and a discussion that took place between Rudolf Steiner and parents at the first Waldorf school, in which Steiner said:

> We achieve nothing in our teaching unless a certain relationship exists between the teacher and child, a relationship of mutual love. That is what we really try to cultivate in our Waldorf School.... We want an atmosphere of love to be alive in every class and for instruction to take place on the basis of this atmosphere of love. But this love cannot be mandated.... But as teachers, we actually need more love than we need for other aspects of our lives. You see, the amount of love people usually have for their children, no matter how many they have is small compared to what a teacher needs. No one has as many children of their own as a teacher usually has to teach in a class.... However, it is absolutely necessary for a teacher to have the same degree of love, although possibly in a somewhat different way for the children in his or her class.... It must be the same love, just as intense.*

This focused my attention on my central assignment and gave rise to the important question, "Where do you find more love?" Just asking this question and asking the spiritual world for help was the turning point. A day or two later, one of my first graders brought in her mother's first-grade main lesson book for show and tell. As she turned the pages, she came upon a song that her mother had learned in grade one, "I Will Go with My Father a-Plowing." It is a lovely

______

*   Steiner, *Rudolf Steiner in the Waldorf School,* pp. 67, 68.

song and I told her that. When I did, she said, "Would you like me to sing it?" which she did perfectly. Then she said, "Would you like me to teach the class?" How could I say no? Soon the whole class knew the song.

A few days later we were practicing our alphabet and singing this same song as the children were coloring in their new letter when the classroom door opened and in came our school administrator with a special guest, the very person who had suggested that I read the book by Rudolf Steiner in the first place, Roberto Trostli. Inwardly, I just had to smile. My class looked like the perfect first grade—purposeful, joyful, quietly engaged, but I knew the truth and I couldn't help thinking that the spiritual world has a wonderful sense for humor and irony.

By the way, there was a second part to the "before school dream." After I couldn't figure out how to get the students in their seats, I turned away. When I looked back moments later, they were all seated, working quietly and creatively. This, surprisingly enough, also turned out to be a foreshadowing of how these students would be as a class—challenging at first, but then creative, cohesive, and a joy to teach.

2

Straight and Curved

In educating children, we will on occasion bring ideas to them that they will understand only later in their lives. This probably occurs most often during the telling of stories. In the dramatic rendering of a tale, we turn the soil of the child's imagination by actively engaging their emotions. Into this fertile inner soil, we drop the seed of an idea that will grow with the children during their lives and hopefully bear fruit in a later season.

Rudolf Steiner repeatedly encouraged the teachers of the first Waldorf schools to do this intentionally. And this is what I have tried to do on the first day of first grade with my four classes, when I spoke to my students for the first time in the auditorium. The story that I have told was given to me by a colleague who served as my informal mentor when I taught first grade for the first time. It is simply called "Straight and Curved." Straight and Curved, the study of form drawing, is the first subject that Waldorf school children encounter in grade one. The story that I told begins:

> The door to the house opened and a mother stepped outside and called to her daughter. "Come," she said, "your little brother is starting school soon and I need you to take him to the shoemaker's shop. When you get there, ask the shoemaker to make him a pair of straight and curved." The girl looked puzzled but the mother assured her, "The shoemaker will understand."

So, the girl took her little brother by the hand, and they walked to the shoemaker's shop. When the door opened, a little bell above the door rang, announcing their arrival. The shoemaker looked up from his work and noticed the children. They, in turn, took in all the details of the shop. The smell of leather and glue, the sound made by the shoemaker's hammer, and of course, the shoemaker himself with his blue apron and his wire rimmed glasses.

The shoemaker peered over his glasses and asked the children if he could help them. The older sister replied, "My brother needs a pair of straight and curved." The shoemaker leaned over the counter to look at the boy's bare feet and spoke. "So, you are starting first grade. Go and take a seat. I will be right there."

The two children sat down and soon the shoemaker emerged from behind the counter with two pieces of leather. One was straight and stiff, while the other was soft and curved. He placed this stiff piece of leather under each of the boy's feet and traced their outline. He then took the supple, soft piece of leather and set it over both of the boy's insteps and traced them carefully as well and told the children that they should come back in two days and the pair of straight and curved would be ready.

The boy was excited to be going to school finally and wanted these new shoes so much. When it came time to return to the shoemaker's shop, he could hardly be contained and raced ahead of his sister now that he knew the way. When he opened the door, the bell rang just as it had the last time. The shoemaker looked up from his work, just as he had the last time. He motioned for the children to sit down. He reached behind him to the shelf and took down a brand-new pair of shoes. The boy tried them on and walked across the shop. They fit perfectly. He was pleased and ready to leave.

But the shoemaker spoke, "You are going to begin first grade and there is something important that you should see. Come."

The shoemaker took the young boy behind the counter and showed him a large, uncovered, wooden box filled with old, worn-out shoes. The boy stepped back. The soles of these shoes had separated from the uppers and they looked like wild creatures with gaping mouths. "Look carefully," said the shoemaker, "You see these shoes. With these shoes, straight and curved have not been sewn together well. You must sew straight and curved together carefully in all you do."

The little boy looked at the shoemaker for a moment, and then he nodded. He would remember these words. He walked out from behind the counter and took his sister's hand. Together they thanked the shoemaker, and the boy opened the door and skipped out into the street, ready for first grade.

This simple injunction, *sew straight and curved together carefully in all you do,* told to six- and seven-year-old children, is also a succinct statement of the educational philosophy of the Waldorf school.

Uniting the opposites

In the last seventy years American education has vacillated between the extremes of straight and curved. Throughout the 1950s and 1960s, education was directed primarily to the child's cognitive development. The lessons contained all the characteristics of straightness. They were direct, predictable, and always had a fixed destination in view. The desks were set in rows; all the writing took place between straight lines; a sharp, definite line was drawn between the teacher and the students.

In the late 1960s this straight aspect was rejected. It was seen as rigid, unbending, unimaginative, all undeniably characteristics of straightness. Desks were moved into circles and semicircles and walls were removed from classrooms. The sharp line between teacher and student became less defined. Education stressed free, unrestricted movement and free, uncontrolled expression.

Then, in the early 1980s, with the report, *A Nation at Risk,* we left the seeming chaos and confusion of the free school and the open classroom and came back to "basics." Programmed learning with scripted reading programs and accountability through standardized tests, products of the computer age, eventually gave education a new appearance. This was a straight line that students were going to follow in a big way. That trend continued with the No Child Left Behind Act, which became law in 2001, and Race to the Top (2009).

Each aspect, straight and curved, is a half-truth. When they are pursued exclusively, education is one-sided, out of balance—we limp along dragging the leg we ignore. It is the goal of Waldorf education to unite these two fundamental aspects in each grade, in each lesson, in each day.

The balancing of these polarities occurs best when education is viewed as an art. It is through the addition of the arts— poetry, drama, storytelling, music, painting, and the creativity of the teacher—that the cognitive material in the lessons is enlivened with spontaneous enthusiasm and joy, so that in sympathy students can readily accept clear, distinct concepts that provide a fundamental understanding of all subjects.

It is the work of Waldorf schools to provide an education in balance. Within each individual, we also find a tendency toward straight or curved. It is the task of the class teacher to know the children, and to know which child has this tendency toward the logical predictability of the straight line and which has a greater affinity for the spontaneity and vitality of the curve. Then they can help the children follow the shoemaker's advice and sew straight and curved together carefully in all they do.

3

Back to the Future

Each morning, when I open the door and step into my first-grade classroom, I immediately feel at home. I like my room—the plants by the windows, the children's watercolor paintings brightening the walls, and the wooden desks and chairs all ordered and arranged to face the blackboard.

I like to think that this classroom is lovelier than the ones I entered as a child, but the truth is that there are strong similarities between this room and the classrooms of my past. Many of today's young teachers would say that my classroom is old-fashioned. It is noticeably lacking the modern accoutrements. There are no tablets or laptops, no white boards with markers, no active board, no CD or DVD player, not even a working intercom. Perhaps I should be worried that I am a dinosaur, some relic from another era when teachers stood at the front of the room and when pencils, paper, chalk, and erasers were all essential ingredients in a school experience. And yet when I read what is being written about education, brain development, and the dramatically changed world that awaits our children, I am absolutely convinced that my Waldorf classroom is leading my students "back to the future."

Several years ago, Thomas Friedman, *New York Times* reporter and author of *The World is Flat,* spoke to a group of students at a highly respected prep school in Washington,

D.C. The students wanted to know what they should do to prepare themselves for tomorrow's workplace. Friedman's answer was striking. He told these students that their education had developed primarily the left side of their brains and that, if they wanted to be prepared for the future, they needed to develop the right side of their brains as well. He told them to "think art, think green, think connectedness."

As it turns out, Friedman's ideas were influenced by what he was seeing in our rapidly changing global economy, in which American jobs were continually being outsourced to countries like India, China, and the Philippines, and by what he had read in a book by Daniel Pink, called *A Whole New Mind*.

In *A Whole New Mind*, Daniel Pink makes it clear that our standard approach to education utilizes only the left side of the brain. This is the education that we are currently promoting in our schools, and Pink states very clearly that it will not prepare our children for the future. If we educate only the cognitive capacities of children, only capacities that can be tested, we are going to make them economically obsolete. Pink cites research that indicates that at least 3.3 million white collar jobs (not to mention manufacturing) and 136 billion dollars in wages have shifted from the United States to low-cost countries like India, China, and the Philippines. Pink also notes that, if we educate children in this conventional way, using only the left sides of their brains, someone in a developing country is going to do what they are trained to do more cheaply, and a computer will do what they were trained to do more quickly. If we truly wish to prepare our students for the future, Pink proposes that we help them develop new capacities in *art, storytelling, play, empathy, finding meaning,* and *symphonic thinking*—all capacities related to the right side of the brain.

What I find reassuring is that these are the very capacities that are being developed in children at Waldorf schools. Art and storytelling are essential parts of the Waldorf experience right from the start of school. When children are taught their letters in grade one, they are introduced to the sounds and shapes of these letters through a story. For example, when they learn the letter "s," a fairy tale about an enchanted snake can be told. In that telling, the students will hear the sound of the snake hissing as it "slithers through the softly stirring grass." On the blackboard they will see a large, colored chalk picture of this sinuous serpent shaped exactly like the letter **S,** which they will draw in the books they create. They will run the letter **S,** paint it, even shape it in modeling wax, all so that they will have a multisensory experience of this and all their letters. But most of all, they will be developing their whole mind.

In her book *Endangered Minds,* Jane Healy underscores the value of this approach to teaching letters.

> All thinking, even language processing, calls upon both hemispheres at the same time.... Since the hemispheres carry on a continual and rapid communication over the bridge of fibers (corpus callosum) that connects them, their ability to interact is probably the ultimate key to higher-level reasoning of all kinds.*

Healy goes on to say that communication between the left and right hemispheres of the brain occurs when language instruction includes picture letters. "People who learn to read both a letter type and a picture-type script, as in Japan, tend

---

* Healy, *Endangered Minds,* p. 125.

to process language more equally between the two sides of the brain than do people who read only letter-type scripts."*

It is not just in the Waldorf elementary school where children are heading back to the future. The Waldorf preschool provides a similar mix of tradition and innovation that is truly in tune with our times. Americans are, generally speaking, an intuitive people, and there are certain assumptions that we innately embrace. One of these is that youthfulness is a desirable trait. Sometimes we go about pursuing youthfulness in puzzling ways, spending millions of dollars on cosmetic surgery and on anti-aging medications. And yet, even when our response is misguided and shortsighted, we clearly sense that it is a sign of health when older individuals still possess a lively, adventurous spirit.

In their book *Geeks and Geezers,* authors Warren Bennis and Robert Thomas note that this quality, which they call *neoteny*—the ability of a species to maintain youthfulness in old age—is often a characteristic of our creative leaders. For instance, the architect Frank Gehry is close to eighty years old, and yet he says that some of his best ideas come to him on the ice when he skates. What we see is that his playful, youthful nature is an important part of what makes him so creative.

Several years ago, the Smithsonian Institution held a conference on the role of play in the lives of geniuses. The conference underscored the formative influence of play in the lives of innovative individuals whose discoveries impacted our society in dramatic and positive ways. One of the unique capacities of scientists such as Albert Einstein, Alexander Fleming, the discoverer of penicillin, and Barbara

---

*   Ibid p. 212.

McClintock, the Nobel prize winning geneticist was imagination. What was clear at the conference was that playfulness and imagination are characteristics of genius.

The wooden sinks and stoves, the natural building materials, the dolls and simple toys all allow young children the creative play experiences that will enhance their problem-solving ability by fostering divergent and imaginative thinking. This stands in sharp contrast to most contemporary preschools, where there is little or no time for creative play and where children are required to work at tables with workbooks, pencil and paper, and computers.

In the Waldorf high school, we are also working to lead students back to the future. Waldorf high schools are small schools with a required curriculum that is both diverse and integrated. Requiring students to take choral music or to play an instrument or to be on a sports team may seem restrictive to some, but these activities are a valuable preparation for the future.

In *The World Is Flat,* Thomas Friedman writes about the educational rebirth that occurred at Georgia Tech. The school's president, G. Wayne Clough, knew that the country needed more good scientists, engineers, and entrepreneurs. He began rethinking Georgia Tech's approach by reflecting on his own experiences working as an engineer. Some of the best engineers he had collaborated with over the years had not been the best engineering students, but they were able to communicate well, relate to others, think creatively, and tie together things from different fields and disciplines. On campus, Clough encountered students with these same characteristics and realized that they tended to be persons with varied interests and activities. They sang in a choir, played a musical instrument, were on an athletic team. Clough encouraged the admissions office to recruit and admit engineering students who had artistic and extra-curricular interests.*

The ability to integrate knowledge and see connections in seemingly unrelated areas has been an emphasis in Waldorf schools since their inception. It is the reason the curriculum is integrated, so that music, for example, is taught in conjunction with history, so that art is part of all science studies, and so that writing is used to enhance the teaching of mathematics.

Daniel Pink calls this integration of knowledge *symphonic thinking*—thinking that asks us to recognize patterns and motifs, to synthesize information, to see the big picture, and to make connections between subjects in surprising new ways. Frans Johannson, in his article in the journal *The Urbanite*, calls this capacity *the Medici effect*, referring to the family that supported a remarkable burst of creativity during the Renaissance of the fifteenth century.

It is this innovative thinking—the ability to connect the seemingly unconnected to create new ideas and solutions—that is at the heart of the kind of problem solving we need for the future. It is this ability that led the architect, Mick Pearce, to design an office complex in Harare, Zimbabwe, that does not need air conditioning. To do this he incorporated into his architectural design an understanding of the way in which termites cool their mounds in the hot, African sun. Writing in the *The Urbanite*, Frans Johannson describes the project:

---

* Friedman, *The World Is Flat*, pp. 312–15.

Pearce's passion for understanding natural ecosystems allowed him to combine the fields of architecture and termite ecology and to bring this combination of concepts to fruition. The office complex, called Eastgate, opened in 1996 and is the largest commercial/retail complex in Zimbabwe. It maintains a steady temperature of 73 to 76 degrees and uses less than ten percent of the energy consumed by other buildings its size. And it saved 3.5 million dollars immediately because [an air-conditioning unit did not need to be installed].*

Clearly, in our era of global warming with the heightened need to reduce fossil fuel consumption, creative problem solving like Pearce's is greatly needed. If we are truly preparing our children for tomorrow, we should be educating them, as Thomas Friedman said, "to think art, to think green, to think connectedness."

So, when I enter my seemingly "old fashioned" classroom each morning, these are the understandings that reassure me. When I teach my first graders their letters through art and storytelling, I do so with confidence that I am stimulating the kind of brain activity that will give rise to higher order thinking. And in fourth grade, when I will watch these same children begin to play violin, viola, or cello, I will rest assured that their ability to think creatively and work collaboratively is being strengthened through music. When these same students, in grades six, seven, and eight, encounter the synthesis of art and science and the love of nature that lived in individuals like Leonardo da Vinci, George Washington Carver, and Rachel Carson, I will hope that these same qualities—artistry, playfulness, and symphonic thinking, empathy, and storytelling—will have been cultivated in them, and that

---

* Johannson, "The Medici Effect," *The Urbanite,* March 2007.

these students will be multidimensional individuals accustomed to using their whole mind in surprisingly new and innovative ways.

4

Developing Good Habits

I knew I shouldn't do it, but I did it anyway. It was just one of those days. I had just brought my class in from lunch recess, and I needed to get them ready for handwork so I could make my way to the eighth-grade room where I was scheduled to teach math. As my students took their seats, I glanced at the clock and knew that, if I arrived at the eighth-grade room late, there'd be a price to pay. So, I greeted the handwork teacher, made sure all of the children were seated and ready, and turned to leave. That was when I noticed the closet and the coats that were all over the floor. A better teacher would have acted differently and called the children whose coats were on the floor to the back of the room and had them hang them up properly. But I was in a hurry, and so I did what I shouldn't have done—I simply closed the closet doors and hid the coats. I had read that every idea that does not become your ideal slays a force in your soul.* But now I felt it palpably, and that feeling would stay with me.

A year later I was with my class in Hawthorne Valley, New York, for our third-grade farm trip. It was our last day at the farm, and the bus was on its way to pick us up and take us all the way back to Maryland. Most of the students had finished packing their suitcases, as time was running short. There was still one boy packing, and his belongings

____

* Steiner, *How to Know Higher Worlds*, p. 25.

were in disarray. His socks, underwear, and tee shirts were strewn on the floor and around the bed. We gathered the runaway clothing and were just getting ready to see if the suitcase would actually close when one of the farm's senior staff, a man named Fentress Gardner, came into the bunk house and looked at the suitcase. "Ah, Jack," he said, "the perfect pedagogical moment—the art of packing a suitcase." I am sure that the look on my face must have said, "You've got to be kidding. I'm just trying to get this boy on the bus." But I knew he was right, and I knew that the next time I came to the farm I would have to do better.

The closest I come to experiencing reincarnation is when I finish an eighth grade. The end of that extended eight-year journey is a time for reflection. My teaching career flashes before me, and I experience regret. I look back over the years, and I am aware of things that I didn't do well in the classroom. This regret, however, leads to resolve, a resolution stating that the next time I take a first grade I will do better.

When I took my next first grade, I wanted to focus on instilling good habits in my students, both in class and on trips. To do this I needed to be much more mindful, and to be sure to allow the necessary time to develop good habits in the right way. But what is the right way? During the preschool years, *what we do* in the presence of young children matters most, for they learn through imitation. In the high school years, *clear thinking* is of primary importance. However, in the grade school, a teacher's feeling life has the strongest influence on the students. The question for me was how could I instill sound habits in the children and do so in a manner that was sensitive and loving, yet still effective.

What I know about myself is that I am a much nicer teacher (and person) when I don't feel rushed. The pressure of having to move a class through a significant transition (for instance the removal of boots and snow pants) with a limited amount of time can make me tense. Even on good days, when I feel rushed there are small but noticeable changes. My teeth clench; my voice has an edge; and I am sure my expression is different. I tighten up. But give me an expanse of time, just an extra five minutes, and I can speak to the children calmly and warmly. I can even watch a child drop his coat on the closet floor and say with a sense of wonder, "Oh my, your coat is on the floor. How did it get there? Please come and pick it up." If I am standing there watchful and yet patient, he will get it right. That exchange is as important for him as it is for me. My mood, which is linked directly to my feelings, can make this teachable moment a time of connection and accomplishment, one that ends with a smile.

I have often thought that there are children in my class (mostly boys) who are "horseshoe students." By that I mean that they seem to believe that you should get a point for close. Hold the coat close to the coat hook, drop the trash near the trash can, come close to finishing a composition carefully, and you should get a point. These students believe that close counts, like in horseshoes. And they hope that the adults will not have the wherewithal and the resolve to dispute this notion.

I take seriously Steiner's statement in *The Education of the Child* that during the grade school years the formation of habits, good habits, is especially important.* I know that, from the beginning of grade one, I have to work to

___

*   Steiner, *The Education of the Child,* p. 23.

establish these habits in a manner that is conscientious and determined, and yet consistent with the principles of Waldorf education. By that I mean to say that I need to be aware that during the grade-school years students are connected to us through invisible threads that connect our feelings directly to theirs. Having sufficient time during transitions allowed me to meet my students with more warmth and patience, and clear resolve. At these times my emotional state needed to be worthy of the children in my class.

Another important opportunity for maintaining a calm and caring demeanor is when responding to surprises. If I could anticipate the challenging moments that would occur in a school day, I was better able to respond calmly.

The First Day

The first day of first grade is filled with promise and importance, but in my experience, it can also be challenging. Having a desire to bring my best effort to my new assignment, I needed to envision what the opening day would be like. At our school there is an assembly on the first day in which each first-grade student's name is called. The child then brings a flower to front of the auditorium and places it in a vase. This vase, which is eventually full of flowers, is a metaphor for the forming of this new class. It is a lovely ceremony but taking the first-grade class to the auditorium on the first day of school can be overwhelming for the students as well as for the teacher. How was I going to prepare my students for this moment? How was I going to prepare myself so that I could picture the start of school happening in a good way and, at the same time, imagine what might go wrong.

I began by recognizing how delightfully excited the children would be on the first day. New clothes, new shoes, a new backpack, a new lunch box, for half the class a completely new school, and for all the students a new teacher. I wondered how many of the children would wake up early, excited, and be a little wilted by the time they finally arrived at the classroom. Getting the students settled once they arrived was paramount, and in that effort I needed help. I asked several of the children's preschool teachers to join me in the classroom that first morning. While I greeted the new first graders and their parents at the door, the preschool teachers would quietly usher the children to their seats and offer them some yarn for finger knitting. The finger knitting would give the students something purposeful and settling to do and we would later use these handmade drawstrings when we made our counting sacks. However, the really important arrangement was that the preschool teachers made sure that each student used the bathroom before the assembly began.

When all of the students had arrived and were seated, I was finally able to speak to the whole class for the first time. It was my job to give them a picture of what was about to occur.

Good morning, children. It is so nice to see you sitting at your desks. In just a few moments we are going to go to the auditorium and the whole school will be there. And do you know why all of the students are there, even the high school?

They are waiting to see you. They want to see if you are ready for first grade and I know that you are.

Soon we will line up, and when we do, we will stand in the back of our room and I want you to imagine that we are standing on a long, straight, golden line. We will stand tall because each of you will have an imaginary golden crown on your head. Then we will leave the room together and walk down the hall-way. When we reach the office at the end of the hall-way, I will stop and look back at you and I am going to see you all standing there quietly, looking at me. No one will need to get off the line to get a drink when we pass the water fountain because we are all going to get a big drink from the water fountain after the assembly.

And when we are seated in the auditorium, we won't be turning around or talking because we will all be look-ing at the teachers who have stories to tell us and we will be listening carefully. Then when it is our turn, I will call your name, one by one, and you will walk to the stage, shake my hand just like you did earlier this morning, place your flower in the vase, and then walk slowly back to your seat. And while we are seated in the auditorium, no one will need to use the bathroom because you have already done that.

The children were wonderful. They listened carefully, waited patiently, and when they were done, they had a drink of water, a hearty snack, and recess. We were off to a good start.

Extra Lessons

It is important to mention that not all of my "best inten-tions" were helpful, nor was I always able to sense what was going to occur.

Another of my resolutions was that I would use the "extra lesson" time that I had with the children outside of main les-son productively. I wouldn't simply give additional recess or free time in the classroom or take out a picture book and read to the class. I wasn't just going to "run out the clock" before lunch or at the end of the day.

During one of these first extra lessons with my new class, I planned to work with the students on their drawing. I was going to help the children draw trees—not just thick trunks with some skinny branches stuck on, but slender trees with roots and strong branches that tapered and thinned.

We were in the midst of this "well-intended" lesson when I noticed that one of my students was crying. I went to her desk to ask what was wrong. "I don't like my tree," she sobbed. I knelt down beside her, spoke words of encouragement, and helped her with her drawing. I was about to give my attention to the rest of the class when one of the boys on the side of the room cried out, "I lost my tooth!" Immediately, the entire class stood up and marched over to his desk. He opened his mouth to show where his tooth had been and the children saw the blood and collectively yelled, "Ooh!" I managed to send him to the office with one of the other boys and was able to get the children back in their seats and working on their drawings.

In a few minutes the two students returned from the front office and the boy who lost his tooth was very pleased. In his hand he held a small plastic treasure box, which our school receptionist gave to all of the children who lost teeth. Seeing the golden treasure box inspired my new first graders. The children with loose teeth, and there were a number of them, began wiggling their teeth with serious determination. Within what seemed like two minutes, another child shouted, "I lost my tooth!" The whole scene repeated itself as if it were part of a script. The children stood up and walked to the desk of the other boy who had pulled out his tooth. He obligingly opened his mouth to reveal the bloody space where his tooth had been. The class gave another collective "Ooh," and I managed to send a second student to the office for a treasure box. Thank goodness it was lunch time, because I was cooked.

When I returned home that afternoon, my wife took one look at me and said, "What happened to you?" I started to tell her, "It was about ten after twelve and I was teaching the children how to draw a tree when one of the children started to cry because she didn't like her drawing and…" She stopped me in mid-sentence and spoke to me in that wise and decisive way that kindergarten teachers have, saying, "Why are you teaching the children drawing at that time of the day? They should be eating lunch. They probably all had low blood sugar."

From that day on, lunch in first grade started at around noon, and I learned that even my best intentions needed editing.

Foreign Language

Over the years I have come to believe that much of what the students do unconsciously in the early grades establishes patterns that continue later on. When those patterns are beneficial, they can pay dividends for years. However, when those patterns are problematic, they can have a negative impact right through the grade school years. I knew that it was part of my assignment to anticipate future challenges and then to work consciously to prevent them.

How many times with my previous classes had I come back to the room after a specialty class and found my students' names on the blackboard because they had misbehaved. I wanted it to be different this time.

An insightful colleague and friend, John Hamann, told me that he believed that children should receive a specialty teacher into their *home* room in the same manner in which we received visitors into their home. Children wouldn't be disrespectful to their aunts and uncles and similarly they should be courteous and welcoming to their other teachers. I liked his idea. I also knew that it was hard for the first grad-ers to sustain their courtesy and attention when they had so many specialty classes right from the start of the year. So, I went to the language teachers with a proposal. Let's limit the number of classes and begin first grade with only one lan-guage and for the first month have the classes be only twenty minutes long. We agreed and I went to the German teacher with a plan.

The following Tuesday when German was scheduled to begin at 11:00, I simply brought the class in slowly from recess and had them use the bathroom, get their drinks, and take their seats. At about 11:15, there was a loud knock at the door. I acted surprised as I opened the door to greet the German teacher.

"Ah, Frau Thorn. Wie geht es Ihnen?"

"Sehr, gut, Herr Petrash. Und wie geht's Ihnen?"

"Mir geht es auch gut."

"Herr Petrash, ist dies die erste Klasse?"

"Ja."

After I had spoken all the German that I knew and had said that this was indeed the first grade, Frau Thorn peeked in the room and the magic began. Over her shoulder she had two bamboo poles. At the end of one pole there was a beautiful sun. The other pole held a lovely evergreen tree. The children's mouths opened wide as they gaped at this surprising visitor with her accoutrements. She then asked me if my first graders would like to learn German. I asked the children that question in English. Oh yes, they said, and so Frau Thorn entered the room and greeted the class. "Guten Morgen, erste Klasse."

I coached the children with their reply—"Guten Morgen, Frau Thorn."

Then Frau Thorn pointed to the sun up at the top of the bamboo pole and said, "Guten Morgen, liebe Sonne."

And the children replied in kind—"Guten Morgen, liebe Sonne."

Then Frau Thorn pointed to the tree—"Guten Morgen, lieber Baum."

And the children replied again with their new vocabulary and newly developing German accent. After this, Frau Thorn led them in a German song and they sang beautifully the way she did. But then she said goodbye.

"Auf Wiedersehen, erste Klasse."

"Auf Wiedersehen, Frau Thorn."

Just like that she was leaving, and the children were so sad. I asked them if they would like Frau Thorn to come back and teach them more German. "Oh Yes! Please," they said.

We were off to a fine start.

5

Morning Circle:
Prelude to an Important Question

The school year was not yet a month old and already I had received calls from three class teachers concerned about morning circle. They were new teachers. Each felt that his or her class suffered when the day began with the forming of a circle for opening activities. They found that the children's attention diminished during circle and that participation became sporadic and, in some instances, minimal. Rather than beginning with strength and unity, the day— these teachers felt—was starting in the wrong way.

Those teachers' concerns closely echoed my own. I don't mind saying that, when I begin a new class, I rarely do an opening circle at the start of the year. I, too, have found that focus and engagement are difficult to achieve, especially in a large class when opening exercises are done in a circle. The mere fact that I cannot look directly at all the children is problematic. We teachers can say so much with our eyes and with a variety of facial expressions that we are able to save our words for when they're really needed. Our direct gaze brings us conscious awareness of what is going on in the class. This is especially important for a new teacher who has not yet developed other organs of perception, such as eyes in the back of one's head.

Circle time is especially difficult for social children. For sanguine children—and in first grade that is a sizable portion of the class—the close proximity of a friend can be almost too much to bear. I have seen children who seem ready to jump out of their skin for sheer joy from having a friend next to them. In such a situation, the children become distracted and main lesson activities become secondary. This is unfortunate because if there is total participation opening exercises can have a magical effect. They can give the class unity and strength of purpose. In a large class, the resulting sense of working together can be especially pronounced, which is why Waldorf teachers like large classes. It is important, then, that the day starts with a positive experience of working together. The teachers who called me, though, were experiencing something quite different when their day began amid the clatter and confusion of moving desks and chairs.

If a main lesson can begin with the children in a circle, all fully participating and with focused attention, then the children are well served. The circle has engendered an experience of oneness. Certainly, there are teachers who start the day having the children move a roomful of desks quietly and gracefully, and the children benefit greatly from having that experience. However, I could not do that in the same way, especially at the start of grade one. So, I chose to start the day in a different manner and yet, I believe, in a pedagogically sound way. Such a decision must rest freely with each teacher. New teachers, trained and untrained, should know that it is possible to do pedagogically appropriate opening exercises without a circle. When I became a Waldorf teacher, my first classroom was twelve feet wide and about forty feet long. The room had originally been three dormitory rooms in a boarding school. With the intervening walls removed, the room was large enough for twenty-four children, but never large enough for a circle. Out of necessity, I had to develop a wide variety of rhythmic activities (clapping, stamping, stepping, chanting, and the like) that children could do standing behind their desks. If we are truly trying to teach children to breathe properly, activities that help this—activities that contrast loud and soft, large and small movements, fast and slow, active and restful, expansive and contractive movements—can be done effectively behind a desk.

With opening exercises, it is essential that teachers be both sanguine and phlegmatic. A class teacher should be sanguine, in that they regularly and joyfully introduce new elements into the opening exercises. The opening exercises can change with the grade, with each new season, or with the start of a new main lesson block. They can even be different on different days of the week. In our class we did extensive rhythmic exercises each Monday, because they were simple activities and assisted "reentry." We did other exercises each Tuesday, because they are more elaborate, more challenging, and require more interaction among the children. I found that my children naturally needed to interact more with each other on a Tuesday. Rather than resist this tendency, I incorporated it into the opening exercises and in other parts of my Tuesday main lesson. The class teacher must also be phlegmatic, in that they repeat certain activities daily over a period of weeks, months, and in some instances even years. There are poems that I taught my class in first grade, which they still enjoyed doing in grade three. These exercises became the backbone, our opening activities. They were done each day and often at the same point in a series of exercises.

With my third class, for example, I decided in grade one to use a poem entitled "Awake, Awake, the Sun is Shining Bright" to start each day. With the help of our school eurythmist, I incorporated gestures to accompany the poem. Each morning we stood and began our day by reciting the poem while doing the gestures. This poem always preceded our morning verse. I hoped that with such a beginning the children would be able to stand up nicely and say their morning verse with more vitality and less slouching. This worked remarkably well until the end of third grade when the nine-year change had begun to have a pronounced effect on my class. I started to see in the children's eyes something that conveyed that they thought this verse was now "babyish." For fourth grade, I introduced a new poem entitled "Straight and Firm on Earth I stand." This poem also had movements, but the gestures were more emphatic and suited older children. My students recited this poem immediately after the opening verse and did that for some time.

Having activity in the beginning of each lesson is always beneficial. However, it is much easier to incorporate activity into a lesson for young children. As classes progress through the grades, opening exercises change dramatically and often focus more on speech and music and less on movement. Still, it is possible with imagination and forethought to metamorphose certain exercises from the early grades into appropriate activities for grades four, five, and six. I have seen teachers modify rhythmic stepping and clapping exercises by using long wooden dowels three feet in length and three-quarters of an inch in diameter. With the use of these dowels, a simple verse such as William Blake's "*Joy and Woe Are Woven Fine…*" can become a rod-passing exercise. This immediately addresses the older students' growing need for social interaction by having them work with partners or in small groups. It also meets the need for more challenging physical activity by requiring the simultaneous tossing and catching of rods. Such an exercise involving twenty or more fourth or fifth-graders in extended rhythmic activity, done with a partner as well as in unison with the entire class, fosters the social cohesiveness that we seek when we use a circle to begin our lesson. Classes who do such exercises clearly enjoy them. When students' needs are met, there is often an enthusiastic response.

I am not saying that the morning circle should not be used. Rather, I am saying that if a teacher feels that it is pedagogically sound to have students do their opening exercises using a different form, then the teacher should be left free to make that decision out of their own intuitive sense of what works best for the class. My concern in this matter grew when I heard from the three new teachers that they felt pressure from more experienced colleague to use the circle at the beginning of their main lesson, in spite of their own sense that it started their day off "on the wrong foot."

We speak of the class teacher time as "the age of authority." Too often, this phrase leads only to discussions of discipline. It should also lead us into a discussion of the originality, authenticity, and responsibility of the teacher. Class teachers are called on to be the *authors* of the work done with the children. This work should rise out of our deep commitment and concern for the specific children in our care. This response must come from our understanding of the students. If we are to be authorities in the true sense, the response to any given situation must be authentically ours, not someone else's.

To meet the specific demands of the situations in which we as Waldorf teachers find ourselves, we must trust ourselves to develop an intuitive sense of what is needed. Out of this inner sensing, the art of Waldorf Education is created anew. This intuitive sense is crucial. It is based on and requires the spiritual activity of the teacher.

To develop self-trust is an important first step for any teacher. What, then, is the second step? It is inner work. When children and parents trust in us, we must depend on what's deepest in ourselves. This calls for an extraordinary response—an inner commitment and dedication to work on ourselves ever more deeply and to call forth that part of us that is our best Self.

Clearly, the question of whether or not to form a circle with grade-school children is secondary. However, the question of whether or not teachers should be allowed to follow their own intuition is primary. We Waldorf teachers should be encouraged to trust ourselves and then to work on ourselves to be sure that the Self we are trusting is our best self, open to the spiritual world. With the necessary inner work, our next step, taken with self-trust, will be even more authentic and more truly our own. But we are still not done. Our actions are like a conversation with the spiritual world. We come to a decision and we act, and then we wait for a response.

The day that this piece was originally published in the journal *Renewal*, I had a most unusual experience. It was just minutes before main lesson, and I was standing in the doorway of my classroom when a student from one of the other classes came skipping by. The child was singing a song by the folk singer Donovan, one that I had known in my younger days. The words I heard and recognized were "Happiness runs in a circular motion." It was clear the spiritual world had acknowledged my thoughts on Morning Circle and then shared some of their own.

6

What if I Were Starting a First Grade Now?

"What matters is not so much a knowledge of abstract educational principles or pedagogical rules. What does matter is that a deep sense of responsibility develops in our hearts and minds." —R. Steiner[*]

When my fourth class graduated, it was clear that my teaching time had come to an end. It had been forty-two years since I had taken my first first-grade class, and the physical demands of the classroom were more noticeable, especially when I worked with younger children. I had gotten older, and the thought of starting over again with another eight-year commitment at the age of sixty-six, stopped me. So, I decided to retire. But the truth is, I will always be a teacher at heart. Currently, I mentor, I help train teachers, and I consult with schools. But when I visit a classroom, I recall the simple joy of spending my day with children, and I miss teaching.

Last summer I was invited to work with the Inklanesh Waldorf School in Mexico City. As I prepared for this work with the teachers, I came upon the following passage: "In real life, the essential point is that you can unfold a certain amount of effectiveness in your actions only if the impulse

---

[*]   Steiner, *Poetry and the Art of Speech,* "Education in the Face of the Present Day" (Oct. 6, 1920).

for this effectiveness is guarded in the soul as a most sacred possession."*

This statement made a strong impression on me, because many times during my teaching years I had felt an urgent need to be a more effective teacher and had made a resolution to become one. I always felt that these moments were important, but I had never guarded them in my soul as sacred possessions. Realizing this gave me pause to consider the "unthinkable" question, "What if I were taking another first grade now? How would I keep alive this awareness of deep responsibility? What would I have to do to keep this understanding in the forefront of my awareness each day?"

Truth be told, I'd had this feeling of heightened responsibility before. In fact, I remember experiencing it at the start of each of my first grades. But sustaining this heightened awareness for eight years proved more difficult. If I had been able to live like Thomas Merton in a monk's shed in nature, my life would have been simple enough to allow ample time for quiet reflection, inner stillness, and sufficient lesson preparation, and I believe that my morning walk to school would have found me in the proper state of mind to meet and work with children. But driving carpool, sitting in traffic, substituting for absent colleagues, attending lengthy meetings, and little by little my best intentions were covered over by the continual demands of the day. Over time, with each developmental change in the students and the disappointments of having students leave my class, those concerns began to hinder my ability to bring my best into the classroom.

Looking back over the years, I see that this is what happened, but I also know that I did what I thought I was

---

* Steiner, *Balance in Teaching*, p. 2.

supposed to do; I did my inner work. I had a consistent, daily spiritual practice. I pictured the children in my class almost every day, I read the *Calendar of the Soul,* and I even did the six supplementary exercises (see chapter 18). Still, I am left with the clear sense that what I did was not enough to keep alive the feelings that illumined and warmed my initial commitment.

I can also see how the emphasis of my work shifted during the class-teaching years from inner to outer activity. In the early grades I worked with the children through stories, painting, poetry, rhythmic movement, and time in nature. But in the upper grades there was a growing emphasis on factual material, and when that change occurred something shifted. It felt as if time became compressed when there was main lesson work to grade, math sheets to prepare and check, science demonstrations to set up, and surprises to encounter. Although I was still able to greet my students with a smile each morning and was grateful for the start of each new school day, the sense that the classroom was a sacred space and that the interaction between a teacher and the students is a destiny laden encounter had diminished. More was needed.

So what would I do now if I were starting over again? I think I would begin with a journal the summer before first grade, where I would try to express, as best I could, what I was hoping to safeguard in my heart when I worked with the children. Then, I would commit to revisiting these statements and, if necessary, adding to them at the start of each new school year. I would also read these entries in early December, when the growing darkness in nature affords us a greater inner awareness. And I would review these statements again at the end of the school year to see if I had been able to remain true to my ideals.

Of course, there would be inner work to do on a daily basis. If there was a quotation that inspired me, I would write it out and place it above my work place at home so I could see it each morning before school to remind myself at the start of the day of what I did not want to forget. Here is one quotation that I have turned to continually: *Ask and you shall receive; seek and you shall find; knock and it shall be opened.*

A Small Story

It was quite late on a Thursday evening, and for one reason or another I was heading to bed without a prepared lesson. I was teaching the third grade Measurement block at the time, and my topic for the next morning was liquid measurement. I was sitting on the edge of the bed ready to lie down, and I had no idea what I would teach the next day. In a casual manner I simply asked for help. Before my head hit the pillow (two seconds?) two ideas instantly presented themselves to me. The first was that I should stage a "liquid measurement" relay race outdoors with water. It was May and the weather was lovely. The second was that the water for the relay race should be dyed with food coloring to make the presentation more beautiful.

That quickly I had the makings of a simple and very interesting lesson. With three desks, three sixty-four-ounce, half-gallon glass pitchers (which we had in our school's kitchen for special events), three clear, eight-ounce plastic cups, and three buckets of colored water (red, yellow, and blue), we were set. I divided my twenty-four students into three groups and asked them to carry their eight ounces of the colored liquid to their pitcher (without spilling any!?) as quickly and as carefully as possible. We would see which group would be the first to fill their two-quart pitcher with colored water and how many children it would take to do it.

This lesson, which took place out on the playground, was lovely. The pitchers standing on the wooden desks looked beautiful in the sunlight as they were gradually filled with color and the children were filled with excitement. It was the perfect Friday main-lesson activity. Perfect. What was extraordinary about this lesson was how markedly different it was from the way I normally taught. I tended to be a more conservative teacher with the usual morning review, book work, practice work, a good story, and artistic activity. But this lesson, so simple in its design, was completely child-centered in its conception, and it was communicated to me in an instant. It was as effective as it was fun! It left me wondering why I had not asked more often for the help of the spiritual world.

During my years as a teacher, I often found the faculty meetings challenging. I was continually discouraged by the conversations and the lack of real listening that occurred and by my role in adding to both of those situations. If I were going to take another class, I would offer to help shape our weekly meetings. I would propose more opportunities for colleagues to speak about their work and to listen to others in a deeper way. One school that I visited, the Paideia School in Atlanta, with a faculty of more than 100 teachers, had a tradition at the start of each school year in which four or five teachers were asked to speak to the theme: Why I teach. These ten-minute talks were inspirational, revealing an aspect of a colleague's deeper commitment to their vocation and to their students than what usually surfaced in the faculty room or out at recess.

We could also incorporate Parker Palmer's work with The Courage to Teach (now called The Center for Courage and Renewal), which supports this type of contemplative practice for teachers. One activity that has grown out of my work with The Courage to Teach uses the poem "Wild Geese" by Wendell Berry. The ending lines to that poem are poignant.

> Geese appear high over us,
> Pass, and the sky closes. Abandon
> as in love or sleep holds
> them to their way, clear
> in the ancient faith: what we need
> is here. And we pray, not
> for new earth or heaven, but to be
> quiet in heart, and in eye,
> clear. What we need is here.*

This leads easily to the question: "What is here at your school that you need?" The answers to this question that I have heard teachers share in the presence of their colleagues have been both profound and uplifting. They were not focused on day-to-day particulars, scheduling concerns, or classroom needs, but instead on the gift of being in a dedicated spiritual community, and on a teacher's profound commitment to their work with children.

Encouraging this kind of contemplative reflection would nourish any teaching community as well as deepen

---

* Berry, *Collected Poems 1957–1982*.

the connection between a teacher and their *better* self, and would help the whole faculty keep the ideals that guide them close at hand.

I believe all of these considerations are important, but the truth is their usefulness is incomplete without something more. I can hold onto the memory of meaningful conversations with colleagues, as well as recall the entries from my journal, and they can serve as needed reminders when I feel discouraged. But simply reading those words and remembering those conversations will not recreate the feelings that I experienced when the realization of deepened responsibility first occurred. Nor will they convey the light and warmth that were part of that original experience, and it is this warmth and light that turns the moment of realization into an epiphany. "Truths acquire meaning in life only when they can be transformed in our souls as a warm feeling, to a light that shines from within us and encourages us along life's path."*

This is where my own spiritual practice would be needed, the contemplative prayer that would be there at the start of each day, my conscious, quiet request to the spiritual world: "Help me to have more love, more patience, more joy, more insight; in short, help me to remember to bring more of your light and warmth into the work I do."

Over the years I have come to believe that teaching should really be like thermodynamics—the movement of light and warmth from within us out into the classroom. This is the awareness that I would want to keep close and guard as a sacred reminder of who and how I want to be when I stand in front of the children.

---

* Steiner, *The Reappearance of Christ in the Etheric,* p. 25.

7

Second Grade: A Hidden Treasure

It was the beginning of second grade and I had just finished telling a well-known Aesop's Fable when a perky and astute student raised his hand. He had been looking at his new watch during the story, the one his parents had given him because they knew I would be teaching the children to tell time that year. When I called on him, he proudly announced, "That story took only two minutes and eleven seconds!" Was it really that short, I wondered?

Like the students, I shared the disappointment that story time, which had been such a vital part of our first-grade main lesson, was now reduced to approximately one–tenth of its previous length. I needed more imaginative material. I just hadn't realized it needed to come from me.

As it turned out, the fables, which I had assumed to be the problem, were actually the solution. Although these stories are a challenge to tell in an extended manner, they are perfectly suited for small informal plays in main lesson, especially since it is easy to rewrite an entire fable as a poem or a playlet that the whole class can memorize.

One of the key ingredients for acting out a play successfully in the younger grades is to involve all the children who are the audience in the performance. This way, the students who are not center stage are involved and invested, not disappointed, disinterested, or distracting. By having the whole class memorize the poem, the students can narrate the entire play and provide the necessary sound effects. This will enable the play to be performed two or three times during a main lesson period allowing for dramatic participation by a larger number of students. Then stories like "The Fox and the Grapes," "The Wind and the Sun," or "The Lion and the Mouse" can be experienced by the children on a deeper level.

Turning our classroom into a stage did not require much more than imagination and a basket of colored cloths. Years ago, I had the good fortune to work with Laura Birdsall, who had taught for a number of years at the Urban Waldorf School in Milwaukee. It was during her years at this public Waldorf program that Laura came to appreciate the importance of drama as a teaching tool. When she and I were asked to design a literacy curriculum for after-school programs in the city of Baltimore, we created The Enlivened Literacy Curriculum, which employed storytelling, art, and drama to promote vocabulary development, writing fluency, and reading comprehension for children from kindergarten to grade three. This project was funded by Baltimore's Safe and Sound Campaign.

At the end of our training program for the after-school staff, each instructor was given a copy of the curriculum and a large Tupperware container filled with an assortment of thirty-inch square cotton clothes in a variety of bright colors—red, blue, gold, yellow, brown, black, purple, orange, green, and white. The cloths came with matching head bands, so that the children could be transformed by their costumes and feel themselves to be a lion, a fox, a tortoise, or a crocodile with a swishing tail.

One of the schools where The Enlivened Literacy

curriculum was being used was in the area of Baltimore where riots had taken place in 2015. It was a rough neighborhood, but like so many of these neighborhoods it was filled with sweet, sincere children. When I visited one of the classes, I asked the teacher if she had done any of the plays that were included in the curriculum. "Oh, yes," she said, "we did "The Lion and the Mouse" several weeks ago. Would you like to see it?" With a nod from the teacher, the children organized themselves in a circle around their desks in a very precise manner. When they were all in place, the first child spoke her lines and the play began. Each child recited a couplet. Once or twice one of the boys missed a cue and the girl next to him would give him a nudge. He'd remember his lines, and the play would continue. These students knew the whole play by heart. They were immersed in the language as well as the story and its meaning. It was a perfect reminder of how effectively drama strengthens learning, while at the same time nurturing character development. When children act out a story, they feel their way into the character that they are portraying and experience on an inner level the ethical and moral lessons that are imbedded in the tale itself.

Yet the fables had even more to offer. These short stories provided continuous opportunities for independent writing. It was always possible to ask the students to draw their favorite part of a fable and then to turn the paper over and write a sentence or two, on their own, about what they had drawn. From there it was a natural progression for the children to begin retelling the story in their own words on paper.

The children in my class had already practiced this when we worked together as a group to write the first fables in their main lesson book. This work drew the students' attention to new understandings such as capital letters and punctuation. My second graders were writing for the first time with both upper- and lowercase letters and needed to know that every sentence begins with a capital and that each proper name does, as well. In addition, talking animals needed quotation marks around what they say, and sentences become more exciting with exclamation points and more intriguing with question marks.

The next challenge, of course, was spelling. "How do you spell ___________?" was asked repeatedly, and I quickly learned to begin our writing time by asking the class which words they would like me to write on the blackboard. I also gave each student a small strip of paper. If they needed to know how to spell a word, they could come to my desk and I would write their word on their piece of paper. If two or three children asked for the same word, I would ask a child to add the word to the list on the board. What I wanted to set in place was a practice where the children would begin to take some active responsibility for their spelling and not simply depend on the teacher coming over to their desk for help. I also knew that many children would rather try to figure out a word or spell it from memory than to stand up and walk all the way to my desk and wait for a bit and that was fine with me.

Still, I needed to do more. That was when I created our "word wall." I used pieces of drawing paper (11 x 17 inches) for each letter of the alphabet, and on those papers, I carefully wrote the hundred or so most commonly used words in the English language, words that the children needed to be able to recognize by sight rather than sound out. For the letter "A," the list included: *about, after, around, always, away, anything. . . .* For "B," there was: *because, before, better, behind, beautiful. . . .* Some letters, like "T" and "W," needed two papers. The word wall allowed me to place more responsibility for correct spelling on my students' shoulders. If a child came up to my desk and asked how to spell the word *nothing,* I could ask what letter the word starts with and then say that it was on the word wall.

When other teachers that I worked with heard about the word wall, they asked me, "Is that Waldorf?" I believe this is a truly important question. What makes something "Waldorf"? What is appropriate in a Waldorf classroom? This question has a number of ramifications. If teachers are enthusiastic and hardworking, if they are working on themselves and have the best interest of their children at heart, shouldn't they be allowed to follow their inner promptings? Isn't that a spiritual activity? Granted there are many good lessons out there and these are shared in the summer classes on how to teach a specific grade. Adopting other teacher's lessons is an acceptable practice and an expression of professional appreciation. But if that is all we use in our classrooms, we establish "Waldorf" cultural norms, and consequently cultural taboos. And when a culture is established too strongly without sufficient variation, it can be perceived as rigid and inflexible, even when it's done with good intentions.

I have always put my faith in certain fundamental principles of Waldorf education and believe these principles should guide my teaching choices. One of these principles is that we should *teach reading through writing.* When I first became a Waldorf teacher, I took that to mean making our own main lesson books and creating our first reader in grade one. It also meant creating compositions together as a class. But as the years passed, I became convinced that children should write their own sentences, as well as brief compositions, before third grade. The fables enabled me to begin this work. The other principle I tried to keep in mind was that, for the grade-school child, the world should be beautiful, so I made my word wall as beautiful as I could. Each letter's sheet was mounted on construction paper matching the color of the writing. And each sheet was taped securely to the painted cinder-block walls in our classroom so they would not fall down or list at an angle. Our rainbow word wall was an artistic addition to our class, one that helped the children learn to spell and to read by writing on their own.

Working with the fables, which started out as disappointment at the beginning of second grade, became an opportunity to expand my capacities as a teacher, another chance to turn lead into gold through the alchemy of Waldorf education.

Here are three examples of the little plays from fables that I wrote for my class and included in The Enlivened Literacy Program.

THE WIND AND THE SUN

The Wind and the Sun were disputing one day
As to who of the two was the stronger.
They bickered and quarreled the morning away.
Their arguments grew longer and longer.
Said the wind: "I am fierce. I am tough. I am wild.
   I am strong.
When my winds are blowing, they howl all day long.
I roar through the valley. I rage through the town.

I turn all the people I meet upside down.
The leaves I make fly. The trees I make sway.
I blow the storms in and I blow them away.
The windows will rattle and the children will hide
Whenever my wild whipping winds blow by."
Said the Sun: "You are strong I am sure
      as none will refute,
But I see a way to settle this dispute.
Let's have a contest for all to see.
The stronger of us, the winner will be.
The contest concerns that man on the road.
The stronger will be able to remove his coat.
So the Sun retired behind a cloud and the sky
      grew dark and grey.
The Wind blew down upon the road and the birds
      all flew away.
But no matter how fiercely the wild wind blew
Around the man down on the road,
It could not remove his scarf or his hat
Or get him to take off his coat.
Then the Sun came out from behind a cloud,
And the day grew warm and bright.
The Sun sent down its gentle rays and bathed
      the man in light.
The man grew warm as he walked down the road
On what was now a sunny day.
He removed his hat and then his scarf
And put his coat away.

THE LION AND THE MOUSE

Once there was a Lion,
A mighty Lion King.
Once there was a Little Mouse,
The smallest little thing.
The Lion was sleeping

Quietly on the ground.
The Little Mouse came creeping.
She did not make a sound.
She ran up to the Lion.
She climbed up on his hip.
She dove into his furry mane,
Then down his nose did slip.
But when she landed on his paw,
She woke the lion up.
He grabbed the pesky mouse at once
And decided to eat her up.
"Oh no, oh no," the small Mouse cried,
"Do not upon me feed.
For I can be an important friend,
If you ever are in need."
"Ha Ha, Ha Ha," the Lion laughed,
"What a silly thing to say,"
To think that one as small as you
Could save a King one day."
So the Lion let the small Mouse go
And he went upon his way.
Forgetting what had happened
Until the fateful day,
When he was caught in a hunter's trap
Hidden near a tree.
He roared and struggled all in vain
But could not yet get free.
Then suddenly he heard the voice
Of a creature very small
Who came to repay a favor
To the Lion, King of All.
"Oh, Lion, I will help
And free you from this trap."
So the Mouse chewed on the ropes
Until she heard them snap.
Then the Mighty Lion

Saw that the Mouse had spoken true
She'd come back to help him
Just as she said she'd do.

The Fox and the Grapes

Delicious and delectable grapes hung down.
Sweet succulent fruit hanging toward the ground.
Juicy and gentle, delicate and special,
Perfectly purple grapes.
Then out from the woods came a creature so sly,
A wily fox with a discerning eye.
He spied the grapes hanging down from the vine.
He leaped and he leaped time after time.
But never a single grape could he taste.
He considered his effort primarily a waste,
And when he left, he turned to say,
"Who cares for sour grapes anyway?"

8

Monday Morning:
Conspiracy in the Classroom

I had seen this look on his face before. Dispirited and pre-occupied, my colleague sat at his desk in the corner of an empty classroom. He was reliving a particularly difficult main lesson. As I approached, he raised his glance, shook his head, and spoke the obvious—"Monday." No more needed to be said.

Monday morning's main lesson presents a unique challenge to the Waldorf teacher. It is a lesson that can be both frustrating and instructive. My own approach to Monday morning was formulated as a response to some disastrous lessons. I had come to believe that there was a conspiracy taking place in my classroom, that the children were working against me. Over time, I realized that, surprisingly enough, conspiracy was exactly what I wanted. However, this was a conspiracy of a different kind, one that I needed to nurture and promote.

In its original form, the word "conspire" means "to breathe together." This is exactly what needs to take place among the elementary-age students in a Waldorf school class. Rhythmic activities, which are vital in making the main lesson lively and pleasurable, have this added benefit. Every poem, song, and recorder piece—every "short, short, long" expressed in clapping or walking—urges the students to breathe as one.

It is not only with rhythmic activities that the children inhale and exhale together. This occurs with the emotional content of the lesson as well. Every gasp elicited in a dramatic lesson fills the students' lungs in unison. Each laugh causes the students to exhale rapidly together. Tears and laughter will leave children breathless, because human breathing and feeling are so closely connected. Feelings are the fertile soil into which Waldorf teachers plant the seeds of many lessons. We work hard to make these feelings shared experiences, to make them part of the conspiracy, the "breathing together."

Yet, come three o'clock on Friday, the unity of the classroom begins to dissolve. The children head home to a variety of schedules and experiences. On the weekend some children are up early, dressed, and ready to help around the house. Others awake slowly, eat breakfast late, and get dressed well after that. Activities vary as well. For some outings to museums, or movies provide great excitement. Other children stay close to home, or visit grandparents, or spend a morning worshipping in a church, temple, or a mosque. Still others are extremely active taking lessons, playing soccer, or riding horses. Clearly the pace of weekend life varies tremendously, and it is no wonder that when children return to school on Monday morning the unity and cohesiveness that usually characterize a Waldorf classroom are often lacking.

To remedy this situation I developed a manner of teaching on Monday that fosters conspiracy—"breathing together." When we had our opening exercises, I added rhythmic counting or additional times table practice and a poem or two from past studies. The effect on the children was more important than what was actually done. Hence, I made the lesson simple and subdued. For instance, in grades three and four I often had the students copy their spelling words. I presented the words methodically, pausing after each and then spelling it slowly. As I did this, I could feel the students begin to settle down and breathe regularly. If we copied a paragraph, which I would usually only do on a Monday, I wrote it slowly on the board so that the fast writers would not race ahead and the slow writers would not dawdle. With a unified pace, the pulse beat of the class became steady. A quiet time for work was always helpful, especially for illustrations. From the looks on the children's faces, I had learned not to talk too much. On Monday morning it is easy to fill the void of our students' listlessness with our own words. I also avoided creative and exciting activities. I wanted the students to breathe in rather than breathe out. If all went well, the class regained its customary cohesion before the morning was over.

This way of working with a class is a special, even exaggerated approach, intended to meet the particular needs of a typical Monday morning. It should be modified if the weekend has been rainy and the students have been confined indoors. If Monday follows a three-day weekend, my approach was again markedly different. My students usually seemed more eager to learn after three days away from school than two.

For me, Monday morning was like a deep breath. It was sobering and quickening, but needed a counterbalance later in the week. By *counterbalance* I do not mean a lack of rhythmical activity, but rather time spent properly emphasizing the individual student instead of the group.

For Waldorf teachers, Monday's main lesson is always a challenge. At times, it can be both frustrating and disheartening, a painful reminder of how much work we still have to do with parents and children. A unity of purpose is a pronounced and recognizable characteristic of a healthy class. Because of this, its absence is felt that much more keenly.

"Classness" is a tangible entity in a Waldorf school. It is fostered by the strong emphasis on continuity and on the rhythmic and feeling element in the lessons.

At the beginning of each week, a Waldorf class needs to be re-formed. This is work a class teacher will take up over 300 times during an eight-year cycle. A good way to facilitate this re-formation is to promote a "Monday Morning Conspiracy" in our classrooms.

9

Third Grade: A Time of Transition

Every Waldorf class teacher has a special grade, a year that is especially filled with magic, wonder, and light. For me third grade has always been that special year. The third-grade students bring a unique blend of innocence and capability. They are energetic, eager, and physically resilient. Unlike older children, they are intimately connected with the world around them. They still inhabit a world where magic reigns, where animals speak, as in Narnia, and where enthusiasm abounds. This enthusiasm is characteristic of third graders. They are eager to take part—to plow, to hoe, to hammer or saw, to thresh or grind, in short, to *do*.

The word *enthusiasm*, the quintessential third-grade characteristic, is derived from the Greek word *enthousiasmos*, which means, "infused with divine spirit." The third graders are still at one with the divine, and a heavenly light still shines in their eyes. They combine the best of both worlds. They are young at heart, connected, and interested in all that goes on around them. They are physically stronger than younger children and more attentive. Third graders stand at a juncture, a crossroads between young and old, between immediacy and separation. In Waldorf education we call this juncture "the nine-year change."

As a Waldorf teacher I have always been deeply grateful to Rudolf Steiner for the guidance he has given us for our teaching. Sometimes I stop and am humbled to think how I might have taught (and lived) had I never encountered Waldorf education. There are so many deep and valuable insights. Often, we observe innovations in modern education that parallel what has been done in the Waldorf school for decades. We see "looping," in which one teacher stays with the same class for a number of years. We see "site-based management," longer class periods, cross-curricula teaching. These are all positive changes in public-school education. But we don't see anything corresponding to the Waldorf school's understanding of a child's inner development. And nowhere in mainstream education do we find any mention of the nine/ten-year change.

From the beginning of his work with teachers, Rudolf Steiner drew attention to this period in a child's life. He showed how this change in the inner life of the child marks the end of the period of imitation, when a child largely replicates what others do and say, and how this change is connected to the emergence of self. At this turning point, the child becomes more distinct and separate from the world. This separation brings a new awareness, the beginning of objectivity, but at the same time a new sense of separation and loneliness.

Steiner observed: *"And the way in which a teacher responds to this situation may be the decisive factor for the child's entire life."**

In Waldorf schools, the teachers are extremely aware of this change taking place in the students at this age. Most

____

*   Steiner, *Soul Economy and Waldorf Education*, p. 166.

Waldorf schools require that children turn seven before or during the first-grade year. Thus, many or most of the children experience the onset of the nine-year change during third grade, although this period of transition does also carry over into fourth grade. Given the previous statement by Steiner, it is natural that Waldorf teachers in the third-grade year feel a great responsibility in shepherding children through this crucial transition. They are continually asking themselves, "What should I do to help my children at this time?" The answer is simple: teach the third-grade curriculum in all its fullness; teach it in as lively and enthusiastic a manner as possible. The curriculum was designed to help children through this important transition.

Perhaps the most obvious way in which the curriculum addresses the nine-year change is through the stories that are told in the course of the year. The stories from the Hebrew Bible offer the children pictures of the beginning of the world. They are wonderful images: the separation of light and darkness, the creation of Adam and Eve, and the Garden of Eden. These are pictures of a time of innocence and harmony, pictures that mirror the inner life of the young child. It is the Fall from Paradise and the subsequent banishment from the Garden of Eden that presages the nine-year change.

It was always striking to observe the children in our school when they saw the Oberufer "Paradise Play."* The play depicts the fall from Paradise, and as the children watched Adam and Eve eat the apple from the tree of Knowledge of Good and Evil they were visibly moved. They'd gasp and call out. Some even covered their eyes. This play depicted outwardly something they were experiencing first-hand.

---

*   See Jacquet, *Christmas Plays from Oberufer.*

Waldorf teachers use the stories from the Bible to teach a wide variety of subjects. The students work with measurement (Noah's ark), the writing of compositions, recitation (the Days of Creation and Psalms), spelling, even grammar, but the deeper lessons, the ones pertinent to the inner life of the child, are by far the most important.

Years ago, I taught a grammar lesson on "doing" words (verbs) with my third graders. I had the blackboard completely clean, and I asked the children to tell me some of the things that they could do. Initially they were slow to respond, as my request puzzled them, but little by little they started to realize what I was looking for. "I run." "I paint." "I sing." "I dance." "I jump… walk… write… throw." And with each new sentence I would write the verb on the board. Suddenly, one child with a mischievous look on her face said, "I kick." The other children understood her meaning immediately, and there was tittering in the class. I wondered what to do. I simply wrote, "kick" on the board with the other "verbs" and moved on. After a series of additional words like hike, sing, laugh, sleep, and eat, there came another mischievous contribution. "I punch." Now the children began to snicker again, but I put punch up on the board with the "doing" words. Before long, the entire blackboard was covered with verbs, nearly a hundred of them. It was a visual tribute to all that human beings can do, a testimony to human versatility.

Then came the surprising educational moment when one child asked, "Why are there so many nice words like sing and dance and paint and smile and then other words like kick, punch, hit, and spit?" And there it was in a simple grammar lesson—a vivid picture of human freedom, a picture closely connected to the Tree of the Knowledge of Good and Evil and of the new awareness brought on by this "nine-year change." The third graders are awakening to the fact that—both in the world and within themselves—good is not the only reality.

Other parts of the third-grade curriculum are also designed to help support the nine-year old. The study of house-building is of great assistance. One feature of the nine-year change is that the children begin to experience uncertainty. They are unsure of their surroundings and begin to worry and to be afraid. The study of house-building corresponds to the third graders' need to find stability in the world in which they live.

In this study, the children begin to see how people all over the world have made homes for themselves on Earth. Through studying the teepee, the igloo, the pueblo, the yurt, et al., the children experience a world where people can provide for their own needs by using their hands and what the Earth provides. This fills them with confidence that they, too, can make a home for themselves here on Earth, that they can confidently put their two feet firmly on unshakable ground.

This confidence is furthered by the study of how a modern house is constructed. The children can feel the solidity of the foundation, the firmness of the floor joists, and the uprightness of the stud walls. They also have a great interest in all that people can do with their hands and are fascinated by the plumbers, the electricians, the roofers, and the painters. They come to sense their own human capability through their class building projects and that they "can do." This feeling is empowering. It works to allay fears and to quell insecurities. At the same time, the children can sense on an intuitive level that their own "house"—their physical body—is being built up in a solid and secure way.

One source of great help in preparing to teach third grade is the book *Encountering the Self,* by a Waldorf teacher named Hermann Koepke. It begins with parents' accounts of changes that take place in children at this age and a teacher's efforts to understand these changes and to help parents understand them, as well. This is crucial work at a Waldorf school, work that should be done well in advance of the actual nine-year change.

Parents will inevitably notice the effects of this change. At home, the children may exhibit new moods and behaviors and/or old ones in an extreme form. They may seem moody, fearful, or solitary. Some will even suffer from headaches, stomach aches, and nightmares. They may no longer be willing to hold a parent's hand or to give a kiss goodbye. The intimacy that existed previously between parent and child can begin to disappear.

Parents will also see changes in the way children respond to school. Enthusiasm, exuberance, and joy may give way to indifference. A heightened individual awareness may lead to a feeling of separation, and children will say that they have no friends, when in fact they have many playmates who enjoy their company. Less inclined to spontaneous and unreserved participation in activities at school, children may complain of boredom. All of this may cause parents to ask: What's wrong? My child used to love school.

Parents need to know in advance that this change is coming and that it is a temporary and necessary stage of child development. It is part of the transition from an experience of oneness with the world to an experience of separate and distinct individuality.

Often, first-grade parents will say, "My child loves school. They want to come to school even when they're ill. You are doing a fine job." I use this opportunity to point out that in a few years, when I will be working just as hard, their child may be responding very differently to school. I mention the nine-year change and say that, at the beginning of third grade we (parents and teachers together) will study this change in the inner life of the child. For this purpose, I share excerpts from *Encountering the Self*.

One of the stories in this book that made a lasting impression on me concerns a young teacher named Gerda Langen. She was observing in a public school and was struck by the contrast between how joyful and vibrant the young children were when they entered school and how ashen and lifeless the older children were when they completed their education. Gerda struggled with two questions: "Is this what our schools do to children?" and "Do I really want to become a teacher?"

> While weighed down by this problem, she explained, I went to a lecture of Rudolf Steiner's and something extraordinary happened. It was as if he turned away from the theme he was pursuing in order to say something about the question that was occupying me. He spoke of a stream that meanders away and vanishes into the ground, only to reappear elsewhere and continue its course. He compared this phenomenon in nature with certain soul developments in human beings. There are forces in the inner life of human beings that also disappear, but then come into view again in a changed form.[*]

---

[*]   Koepke, *Encountering the Self,* pp. xiii, xiv.

This happens with our children in grades three and four, and then again in the later grades. It is supposed to happen. But those forces are not gone, rather they are under the surface like an underground stream and it becomes the teacher's assignment to tap into these forces through their lessons.

In reading *Encountering the Self*, I was also struck by the role that farming can play in helping the children find a sense of security. I was so taken by the notion that our solid, bountiful Earth gives this reassurance to the children, that I taught farming as the first block in third grade. Even though our farm trip would not come until the spring, I wanted the children to experience the bounty of a harvest.

We went as a class and picked apples for the whole school Michaelmas celebration at the end of September, and when we stood in the orchard looking at all the apple trees laden with fruit, it gave the children a deep sense of wellbeing, such as that given by a well-stocked pantry before the coming of winter. We picked apples; we cored them; we sliced them; we hung them in our room to dry. We also harvested sweet potatoes at a local farm. The children followed the potato digger and unearthed the potatoes as if they were treasures hidden in the earth. Each child lugged a heavy drywall bucket full of sweet potatoes from the field. When we looked back at the field, there were still so many sweet potatoes drying in the sun that you couldn't even tell that hundreds had already been taken away. The children were able to experience the wonderful bounty of our Earth, and I knew that this experience would be a healing medicine for the discomfort that "the nine-year change" would bring.

The farm trip, as well, provides children with quiet confidence for this new phase of their life. For many children it is the first time that they are away from home without their parents. They have to unpack and pack their bag, make their beds, clean their rooms, clear the table, and eat some of everything that is put on their plates. Each day during the week at the farm, they are called on to work, to muck out the barn, to gather eggs. In short, they are asked to be grown up. Rising to the occasion fills the children with a sense of self-worth, which dignifies and ennobles their newly emerging sense of self.

There is so much in the third-grade year that is memorable. It is a year filled with projects—painting murals, baking bread, planning and building a structure—and with growth. The children at the end of the third grade are quite different physically and emotionally from the way they were in September. They are no longer young children. You can see this change in their eyes. There is more reserve than there was in the fall, but also a bit more self-awareness, more clarity about the human being the child is trying to become. The third graders are now students ready for the challenge of the coming years. They have come through a major change in the way they view and relate to the world in which they live. We hope that, with the help of the Waldorf curriculum, they will be standing firmly on their feet, filled with enthusiasm for this life that they are now beginning to see in a new way.

It was a regrettable day in my third-grade classroom. I had been unbelievably grumpy. That afternoon I was in a gift shop and I saw this gargoyle and thought, "That was me all day. I don't want to be that teacher!"

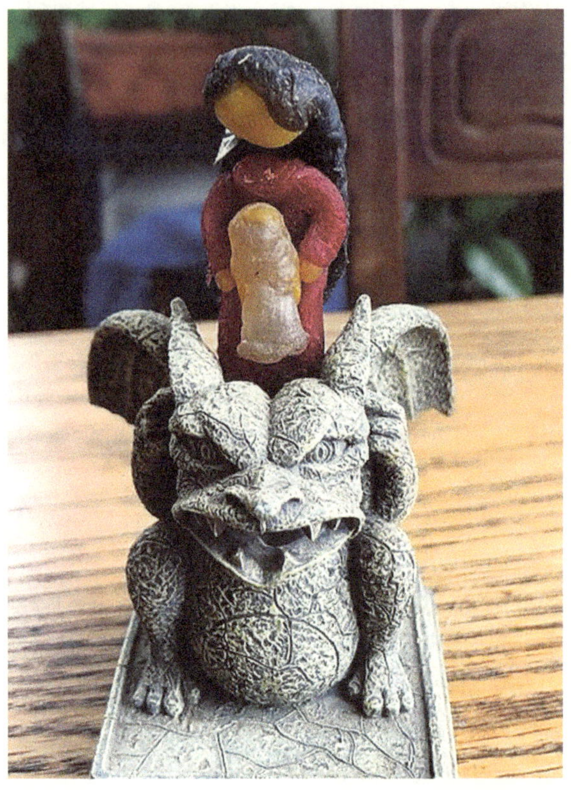

So, I purchased the gargoyle and placed it on my desk to remind me to be nicer. A few days later one of my students secretly added the beeswax figures to redeem the gargoyle (and the teacher). They stayed on my desk until the last day of eighth grade.

10

Deepening Our Work

An unexpected email was in my inbox. It had come from the director of the Institute for the Future of Education. Julie Wilson and I had met several years before and she wanted to speak with me about education in the aftermath of school closings and virtual learning. It was during our conversation that Julie Wilson asked me a surprising question: "If Rudolf Steiner were around today, what would he say we should be doing in our schools, given the pandemic?"

This was a great question, but I didn't have an immediate answer. I deferred and asked if I could think about this further and get back to her. A day or two later I woke from a dream in which I was asked another question: "What is the value of a liberal-arts education?" This question, however, seemed to be covered with dust the way old books are when they haven't been taken off the shelves for a long time. So, I got up thinking that I would write an early-morning email to Wilson and, while doing so, remembered that a liberal-arts education was designed to help students understand what it means to be human through the study of a wide array of subjects.

The idea of cultivating a deeper understanding of our humanity seemed important now, but clearly our current times, with the pandemic, the fires out west, and our rapidly changing climate needed more than yesterday's dust-covered education. This brought me back to Julie's original question, and now I had the beginning of a response, so I wrote:

> I believe that one of the things Steiner would say (because he said this back in 1917 in the midst of World War I) is that "We are challenged to do everything we can to encourage spiritual life as the only way of freeing humanity from destructive forces."*

Then I continued to say that I don't usually quote Steiner like this, but I was recently in a book group with a number of friends and we had just read this statement. Spiritual awakenings are not easy to picture, but I think that what Steiner is saying is the same thing that Vaclav Havel said when he addressed Congress back in 1990.

> The salvation of this human world lies nowhere else than in the human heart, in the human power to reflect, in human modesty, and in human responsibility.
>
> Without a global revolution in the sphere of human consciousness, nothing will emerge for the better... and the catastrophe toward which the world is headed, whether it be ecological, social, demographic, or a general breakdown in civilization, will be unavoidable.**

This global revolution in the sphere of human consciousness is exactly what Rudolf Steiner hoped for when he created the first Waldorf school in 1919, in the aftermath of World War I and in the midst of the economic turmoil that was taking place in Germany and in Russia. But for Waldorf schools today the question persists: "How do we educate

---

*   Steiner, *The Fall of the Spirits of Darkness,* p. 28.

** Speech to the U.S. Congress, Feb. 22, 1990; see https://www.vhlf. org/havel-quotes/speech-to-the-u-s-congress.

children to foster a spiritual awakening?" This is a complex and delicate matter and our response must take place in a number of ways.

Ted Sizer, the founder of the Coalition for Essential Schools at Brown University, wrote that the essence of a school lives in *the surround*. "The surround" is formed by the intentions of the teachers and the administrators, what they hold in their consciousness regarding the work they are hoping to do with the children in their care. It is shaped, as well, by the founders of a school and the very reason they began their school in the first place. This surround is what we feel as parents when we enter a school, step into a classroom, and sense that it feels right and say to ourselves, "I know this is the school for my child."

The surround is like the air we breathe. It is something the children take in each day, and it is sustained by the ideas that are behind the work in the classroom and how those ideas take shape in the day-to-day practices. In a Waldorf school, it is determined by the reverence the teachers afford to the mystery of each child's life and what it means to work with children in developmentally appropriate ways. It is at the heart of what lives between a teacher and a child, that essential relationship. It is also about what lives between a teacher and the students' parents, and what transpires collegially among the teachers. In a Waldorf school it is about the earnest yet modest striving of the faculty, the quiet inner work that goes on behind the scenes.

This spiritual awakening is never about preaching. But it is about a teacher's effort to plant seeds for future awareness, seeds that will take root and sprout in the inner life of the student at a later time, and these seeds are planted differently with each child and by each teacher. Yet, as every gardener and farmer knows, it is not the sowing of seeds that matters most; it is the preparation of healthy soil.

In a Waldorf school the teachers focus continually on this "soil" health. When the early childhood teachers work with young children, they know that the child's experience of the physical world makes a deep impression: the sun's warmth, a bird's song, the wind rustling the leaves of a nearby tree all delight children. It is the same with the experience of a parent's soothing voice when they are held and comforted. All of these simple experiences make a strong impression on the young child, as do the words, gestures, and purposeful actions of the adults, which children see and imitate.

The preschool classroom is designed to have the soothing atmosphere of a home. The children are nourished by the color of the room, the ambient lighting, the healthy snacks that the teachers prepare each day, the creative play, the sound of the singing, and more. These early childhood experiences in the classroom and out in nature help to develop vitality in children, and a strong healthy body provides the children with a solid foundation for life.

As the children grow older there is more to do. In the grade school, the teachers' work shifts. Now they are engaged with the emotional and imaginative life of the student as the inner life deepens and matures. This affective aspect of a child's education takes place in a variety of ways. It is enhanced through long-term relationships. Placing students in a class configuration where they will stay with the same classmates for eight, twelve, sometimes fourteen years (nursery through high school) helps to create a learning community in which the students will become accustomed to learning from one another collaboratively.

The students are also connected to a community of teachers who will know them for years, teachers who will watch them grow and evolve into adolescents and by senior year, into healthy young adults. The teachers will understand their learning styles, their gifts, and their challenges—how they seem when all is well, but they'll also notice when a child's demeanor seems to indicate that they are not quite themselves.

The students' inner lives will be nourished through a rich and varied curriculum that is designed to reflect the developmental changes that occur as they mature. Students will be encouraged to be emotionally responsive to the subjects they study, and that process will be enhanced by incorporating the arts into the lessons. Poetry, drawing, drama, painting, music, and modeling are employed to enliven the lessons in hopes that the students are inwardly engaged by the world they encounter.

Beginning in the middle school, the curriculum shifts to address the students' thinking more rigorously. Developing thinking is an extended process and although this work is emphasized in the upper elementary grades, it intensifies in high school.

Several years ago, a graduation speaker at our local Waldorf school told a story about her son who had transferred to our high school at the start of his junior year. He had attended a well-respected prep school in Washington, D.C. After six or so weeks of school, he told his mother, "I don't know how much you are paying for the Waldorf school, but I think you are wasting your money."

"Why's that," the mother asked.

"Well, we just finished our study of *Hamlet,* and you know what my English teacher asked me? What do you think?" he asked.

"Oh," replied the mother, "that's probably just Mr. Hall."

"No, Mom. They're all like that. They all want to know what I think."

I found this story to be a wonderful confirmation of the good work that can be done in a Waldorf high school. I imagine that at this student's former school his teacher noted all of the important information about *Hamlet* on the board: Shakespeare's longest play, a tragedy set in Denmark in the thirteenth or fourteenth century, the main characters—Hamlet, Claudius, Gertrude, the Ghost, etc. The dutiful students wrote down the important information and studied for their test. But did they grapple on a deeper level with the key ideas in *Hamlet* like revenge and depression, suicide, and duplicity? I have heard on a number of occasions college professors bemoan the fact that students today are not eager to think their own thoughts but instead seem only interested in what they have to do to get an "A."

In the middle school and high school, the students' thinking is strengthened through writing. Whether they are detailing precisely their observations of a science experiment or writing an essay on a topic in history or English, or listening carefully to their classmates in a seminar discussion and responding thoughtfully, they are developing their thinking. And with this newly developed thinking comes a growing sense of who they are becoming, a growing sense of self.

Several years ago, I attended a gathering with a number of professionals and academicians. This gathering was convened by the Mind and Life Institute and arose out of a request by the Dalai Lama who wanted to develop a curriculum for students that would promote compassion and empathy. There were university professors in attendance from the fields of neuroscience, philosophy, religion, education, and psychology. Each spoke, but it was a psychology professor who captured my attention. She stated that for years psychology had determined the accepted picture of the human self. In the early part of the twentieth century this was influenced by Freud, and his image of the self was focused on subconscious urges. After Freud, B. F. Skinner, in his behavioral approach to psychology, characterized the human self as determined by conditioned responses. Next the physiologists contended that all human thought and emotion was a byproduct of the chemicals that were produced in the brain. And today our human self is seen as a computer. We are *hardwired* to act in certain ways as we *download information* with our *limited bandwidth* and our *default responses*. What she then went on to say was that we needed a new picture of the human self, one that is deeply connected to everything around it and is truly collaborative with nature, rather than competitive.

This new picture of the human self is the seed that we should be planting continually through our work with our students. Teachers are encouraged repeatedly by Rudolf Steiner to connect what we teach in science to our understanding of the human being. This can occur in a zoology lesson, which is described in detail in the following chapter ("Fourth Grade"), or in a botany lesson in fifth grade when we teach the students about the jack pine. This amazingly resilient tree releases its seeds only in the intense heat of a forest fire. Our human nature is such that we are like the jack pine. There are dormant forces of renewal within us that are often released when an unexpected crisis occurs in our lives.

In high school botany, we should also introduce our students to the work of Suzanne Simard, the botanist whose study of the forest floor has given us a new awareness of the interrelatedness of the tree community. Simard's studies detail how the root systems of the forest trees are deeply intertwined and how they are interdependent. They share chemicals like phosphorous and nitrogen, and the older *mother trees* in the forest supply smaller trees with carbon that the saplings are not able to produce through photosynthesis because the tree canopy is too dense to allow the light to reach them. These forest communities are collaborative, not competitive.

As human beings we are able to choose the moral or amoral compass to direct our lives. We can decide to be connected to others or we can remain isolated; we can choose to be collaborative, not competitive. We can do our work for the good of others or we can work solely for ourselves. The choice and the balance we choose is ours to determine, but it is influenced in a significant way by our picture of the human being.

This image of the human self can even be brought to children in first grade through the telling of fairytales from around the world. I know that fairytales are not popular today for a number of understandable reasons, but they offer much-needed insight into our human nature. We repeatedly encounter creatures—bears, foxes, even beasts—in these old stories that have been transformed by enchantment. It happens in these stories that something occurs to reveal the creature's true nature. In one story, a great bear visits the forest cottage of two sisters. Upon leaving, the bear catches its fur on the door latch and the fur tears. When the two girls look, they can see gold shining beneath the fur. At these moments, the children experience this being's hidden higher nature. We also have within us something dignified and noble. Children need to understand that, in spite of the beastly things they see people do in the newspapers and on tv, there remains something within us that is golden.

As human beings we inhabit two worlds—the earthly and the heavenly. We stand with our feet on the earth at home in the natural world. As Earth citizens we have a responsibility to our planet—to the soil, the air, the water, the plants, the animals, and to each other. But at the same time, we must nurture our connection with the spiritual world. That is why we begin each day in a Waldorf school with the morning verse, a reminder of our twofold human nature, the inner as well as the outer. Waldorf teachers are called on to hold within us an awareness of the higher nature of human existence. This is the surround students need. Will they be able to make sense of the world and of their lives without turning toward the spiritual world in contemplative reflection and meditation? And without an awareness of their higher nature will young people be able to find the resilience to weather the trials that they are bound to face? Our challenging times are asking more, requiring that we deepen our work to promote a spiritual awakening, both in ourselves and in our students. This, I believe, is what Rudolf Steiner would urge us to do if he were here.

Fourth Grade:
After the Nine-Year Change

It was the perfect fourth-grade question: "Who is the fastest runner in the class?" The hands shot up. I knew they would. Fourth graders divide their class like fractions into a wide array of categories, the fastest runner being just one of them.

"Nathan" was the first answer that came from the students, and there were nods of agreement throughout the classroom.

"Who's second?" I asked.

"Adia is the second fastest." Again, there were nods of agreement, no dissension.

"Third?" I continued.

"Cameron," they said.

"Okay," I responded, "if I were to ask Nathan to stand outside the window of our classroom and, when I say 'Go,' to run across the blacktop, touch the fence, turn around, and run back, how long do you think it would take?"

The students thought for a few seconds, and then the hands went up again.

"Sixty-five seconds," one student suggested.

"No, that's too long," came an immediate reply.

"Forty seconds."

"Twenty-seven seconds," an exacting student offered.

I wrote all of the times up on the board and then said something that I knew would make this lesson memorable. "Nathan," I said, "I want you to climb out of the classroom window and, when I say 'Go,' run across the blacktop, touch the fence, and run all the way back. But first, who has a watch with a stopwatch?" (There is always a fourth-grade child with one of those!)

Nathan climbed out the window while envious classmates looked on. He waited for his signal and raced across the playground and was back in thirty-two seconds. Adia went next. Her time was thirty-five seconds. Cameron was third. His time was thirty-seven seconds.

Of course, I knew I was about to disappoint the rest of the class. Surely there were more students who wanted a turn, both to run and to climb out the window, but we needed to move on. I had a lesson in mind, and all of this was just the beginning.

I started my Waldorf teaching career nearly forty years ago, and I can't always remember where I get my ideas for lessons. So many conversations have faded in my memory that I have started to think that these ideas are mine. But the lesson I wanted to impart this day I knew had originated with Dorothy Harrer.

Dorothy Harrer was a master class teacher for many years at the Rudolf Steiner School in New York City back in the 1950s and '60s. Her imaginative and effective methods of presenting the Waldorf curriculum have been preserved in a series of books on teaching arithmetic, English, history, and other subjects. The lesson I was planning to use in our fourth-grade study of the eagle came from Harrer's book *Nature Ways in Story and Verse*.

Now I was ready to ask my students the next question. "Can anyone think of a way to get to the fence and back more quickly than Nathan or Adia or Cameron?" I scanned the faces of my students, and I could see by the look on Steffen's face that I had not been precise enough with my question.

"But you cannot use a machine," I added.

Steffen sighed with exasperation. He had been thinking "motorcycle." However, his spirits revived instantly.

"Bicycle," he said.

He was disappointed when I informed him that the bicycle is also a machine even though it doesn't have an engine. Now the rest of the class was puzzled as well.

Then Gretchen, a quiet girl who sat in the back of the room, calmly raised her hand. When she answered, I realized once again how perceptive and thoughtful these quiet children can be.

"With my eyes," she said, "I can look at the fence and look back to the school instantly."

I smiled and said to her, "But what if I had asked Nathan to run all the way down the hill to where the first grade plays at recess? What if I asked him to go to a place that you couldn't see? How could you get there quickly?"

There was a pause, and then Pammy, a thoughtful child in the back of the room, raised her hand.

"In my imagination," she said. "In my imagination I could go to the first-grade playground and back in an instant."

Now we were at the place where we could really begin Dorothy Harrer's lesson. I asked the children to close their eyes and to imagine that they were all outside the classroom, as Nathan and the others had been. Then I asked them to imagine themselves in the air above the school, something they had done when they had made their map of the school grounds during our study of local geography earlier in the year.

"And now," I said, "picture yourself flying west above the blacktop. Look down; there are the basketball courts and the trees by the first-grade playground. Let's cross the Potomac River; now we are over Virginia. Look up, you see the mountains in the distance. Those are the Blue Ridge Mountains. Let's keep going."

I continued to describe our imaginative journey across West Virginia, Kentucky, Ohio, Indiana, and Illinois—states that, as I told them, we would study in fifth grade. We crossed the Mississippi River and looked down on the Great Plains. Finally, we could see the Rocky Mountains in the distance. From this point on, the lesson was pure Dorothy Harrer:

> Let's let our quick, wakeful thought make its way, now in an instant, to the high mountain cliff that rises up above the prairie way off to the west, farther than the eye can see or legs can run. Let's go to the rocky ledge, like a platform, where the storms have made the rock break away. Far below us lies the prairie. Far above rises the top of the cliff. Here on the ledge, we find that a bird has its dwelling, which looks like a giant robin's nest. Sitting in the nest are three strange-looking young birds, already bigger than any robin. We hear the sound of wings beating the air. As we are here only in thought, we are invisible, and the great bird that soars down to the nest doesn't even see us. And life goes on as if we weren't there at all. The bird has a body almost as long as (Neal) is tall. Its wings spread out so far on each side that we could lay a yardstick down three times from one wing tip to the other. Now we know that it is an eagle.

In its great, hooked claws the eagle carries a fat, but lifeless, jackrabbit. This it lays before the young birds, who crouch and spread their small wings and utter squeals of excitement; but they still do not approach the rabbit. The mother bird then stands on the dead rabbit and with her strong, hooked beak begins to tear it into pieces, swallowing some herself and passing some with her beak to the beaks of her children. Each one of the eaglets patiently awaits his turn. It isn't long before the rabbit has disappeared entirely.

Just as the meal is over, the father eagle soars down from the blue sky, carrying on one foot a dead mole, which he soon disposes of with a few sharp strokes of his beak. Then, as the mother settles down and draws her eaglets under her great wings, the father perches on the rim of the ledge. He scans the sky as if on the lookout for any enemy that might sail down upon them. He peers downward toward the prairie as if to spy out another meal moving among the grasses below. *

As I describe the eagle lifting and rising on the warm air currents, I tell the children how the eagle is a kin of the air, how it has small air-filled sacs within its body, how its feathers have air within them, how even its bones contain air. I describe how, as the eagle rises high above the land, it can, with its keen vision, spot prey hundreds of feet below. "The eagle," I say to the children, "has remarkable eyesight. I have been told that if an eagle could read, it could read a newspaper from a quarter of a mile away." When I finish saying this, I describe how the eagle draws in its wings and plummets toward the earth like a bolt of lightning, grasps its prey with those sharp talons and carries it away.

---

*   Harrer, *Nature Studies for the Elementary Grades*, pp. 24–26.

Finally, I say to the class, "Do you know, children, how you are like an eagle? It is in your thinking that you can see so clearly. It is in your thinking and your imagination that you can soar to such heights and move from one place to another in an instant. It is in your thought-filled, wide-awake mind that you are like eagles."

That was my moment of insight, and I wondered why it had been so long in coming. In a Waldorf school our primary task is helping children understand what it means to be a human being. We teach many subjects and develop a wide array of capacities, but understanding what it means to be human is the underlying aim. I realized that above our school entrance there hangs a sign, written in invisible letters, like the one in Plato's Academy: "Human Being, Know Thyself." Of course, that is what a Waldorf school would offer its students.

I had started out to teach the children about the eagle. But, in the end, they had also learned something about themselves, that in their capacity for imagination and thought, they have the power and strength of that magnificent ruler of the skies.

I 2

The Heart of the Matter

Waldorf teachers are like dowsers. We move through our teaching days with our students, trying to sense the essential educational ideas that underlie what we observe in our classrooms. When an educational idea gets our attention, causing our dowsing rod to dip, our work begins. Then we start to dig, hoping to unearth a wellspring. When we truly penetrate a pedagogical principle, it bubbles up much the way a spring does, bringing life to everything around it. Similarly, as we work in this way our teaching comes alive. But it does this in a truly individual manner. In freedom, we choose the ideas that mean the most to us and through our earnest inner work they shape our teaching.

For me, one important principle has been the three stages of child development: birth to around seven, seven to fourteen, and fourteen to twenty-one. What I have always understood from this picture of child development is how differently the needs of children manifest during each stage.

When I pay careful attention to this picture of child development, I am reminded that my work in the classroom will need to evolve over time. There are two significant nodal points of change during the eight years of class teaching and each of these developmental changes can affect my relationship with my students. One nodal point occurs between nine and ten, as discussed in chapter 9, and the other begins around twelve and will be addressed in chapter 17. These times of change present unique challenges for teachers. A number of the habits that have been established in the beginning years will be called into question as students develop a stronger sense of self-awareness. I need to remind myself that these changes, although problematic at times, are an important part of children's maturation. They are not an aberration, but rather essential transitions on their journey.

At these junctures, our teaching needs to change as well. Even if we have done an excellent job of instilling good habits in the first three grades, we will still find our students behaving in ways that will surprise and sometimes disappoint us. What should not change, however, is our warm and measured emotional response to all that arises.

During the first three grades, my students had been using the restrooms independently without an issue. At our school it is not a long walk to these facilities. Even the adventurous children could make it back to the classroom without a mishap. At some point in the early grades, some of the boys noticed—initially with outrage and then with growing interest—that a number of the older children at our school fooled around in the restrooms, and that on occasion they climbed on the stalls and ran the sink water at full force, splashing water onto the floor.

With the nine-year change, some children just cannot help themselves. The day did come in grade three when my students also turned on the water forcefully, soaked paper towels and then threw those soggy towels at the walls, the mirrors, and the ceiling to see if they would stick. These shenanigans were accompanied by raucous laughter. It was an exhilarating experience until some of the first graders informed the office staff and this information was brought to my attention.

At a moment like that, there are things I should not say and ways in which I should not say them. But most of all I shouldn't think, "That couldn't have been *my* class." I should not be surprised because, if I am, if pride gets in the way, I am sure to overreact. However, when I remember that this type of behavior is "normal" and that it is brought on by the nine-year change, I am better able to remain calm.

So, when I found out which boys in my class were responsible for the mess, I was able to calmly go with them to the bathroom and survey the damage. If I was really at my best that day, I might even turn to wonder and be amazed by the fact that wet paper towels actually stick to the ceiling. But at the same time, I'd be thinking that it is going to take all recess to clean this up and if it takes some of their next recess as well, that's fine. So, we gather the necessary supplies: a broom, dust pan, a putty knife, a ladder, some cleaning cloths, and we are ready to work. In the end I am hoping the children have taken away two important lessons. The first is that their teacher still likes them and the second is that through their effort they have been able to make things right.

This whole episode was emblematic of the nine-year change. No parents needed to be spoken to. No compositions or apology letters needed to be written—nothing out of proportion. The good habits that had been established were called into question and were reestablished with caring and consequence and the understanding that we clean up our messes. The latter, in and of itself, is a worthy twenty-first-century lesson.

In my years as a teacher I have come to appreciate the small voice inside me. At moments like these, that inner voice has been known to ask, "What would St. Francis do?" St. Francis is the name I insert. It could be Buddha, Mother Teresa, or Gandhi or... But what I imagine is that any of these individuals would be loving. If paint spilled on the floor in St. Francis' classroom, I believe he might say, "Oh my, look at that. What a beautiful color." Then after appreciating the sight, he would add, "But our building manager, Mr. Cox, might not like this color on the floor as much as we do. We had better clean it up carefully. Let's get some warm water, some soap, and cloths..."

At some point during first or second grade in my last class, I had an epiphany, and I really don't know why it took so long. My wife would always ask me how my day was when I saw her after school. My realization was that, no matter what had occurred during the day, if I met the challenging moments with my best self, it was usually a good day.

It is the beginning of fourth grade, and I am at our class picnic in a park near our house. After eating lunch and speaking with parents, I am standing on a small hill looking down on a large open field. Some of the girls in my class are walking the perimeter of the field, and it immediately strikes me that they are thinking of wandering off into the woods. Then I realize, "Of course, this is geography."

The Waldorf curriculum has served me in many wonderful ways over the years. One important way is that it has given me deeper insight into the inner life of my students. The fourth-grade curriculum has been designed for students who have now gone through the nine-year change and one of the new subjects introduced at this time is local geography. This subject is taught to the students with the understanding that their world is expanding and that there are boundaries that they are wishing to cross.

Our school playground has a similar wooded area bordering the playground, which is the official boundary for the children. Something told me that these same students, whom I had seen walking the perimeter of the park where we had our picnic, were getting ready to cross the same kind of boundary at our school. My job was simply to be there when it happened. One day, as the class came in from recess, three of the girls were missing. I knew just where to look, and because I had seen this coming, I was able to avoid some of the ridiculous statements that I can make when I am worried about missing students or bothered by students who are late to class because they claim that they didn't "hear the bell."

Fortunately, I could speak calmly and thoughtfully. My blood pressure had not risen at all. "Girls, where were you? I was looking for you everywhere and I was worried. What if something happened to you? How would I know? You know that your parents expect me to watch over you and to know where you are. What would I tell them? I don't want to worry like that again so you are going to need to stay close to me out at recess. Where I go, you must go as well."

During the first recess it was fun for these students to follow me around like giggling shadows wherever I went. By the second recess it wasn't quite as much fun. They asked, "Can we go play now? We won't go into the woods again."

I have felt on a number of occasions that when children knowingly do something they shouldn't, there should be a reasonable consequence and that a reasonable consequence should become their pain. Once the girls lost their enthusiasm for following me around the playground, the consequence had raised their awareness. If I had been upset, what transpired would have been about my pain, and that would have clouded the whole interaction, focusing attention on my response rather than on what the girls had done. If I had resorted to an extended lecture, it would have been just so much talk and it would have gone in one ear and out the other. The old adage, "Actions speak louder than words," applied here.

I am often struck by how complicated disciplinary situations can be. Some years back I was visiting a class that was preparing for a class play. It might have been a fifth-grade class. There is often a time in almost every class-play production when the teacher feels that the play is going to be an unmitigated disaster. The students don't know their lines; they don't know where to stand on stage; and the students backstage are fooling around. After a restless night's sleep, a disheartened teacher often comes to school with new resolve and "means business."

Unfortunately, this teacher that I was observing had to "mean business" on a day when she had been scheduled to have a visitor in her classroom. When the class went to the auditorium, she set out the ground rules. "No scripts on stage." "And absolutely no talking when you're not on stage." The play practice proceeded, and after a few minutes it was clear that the play was progressing nicely. Then two of the girls seated near the teacher turned to each other and began assessing the other's appearance. They touched each other's earrings and quickly mouthed their approval. Then one of the girls began braiding her friend's hair, and as this continued they had a quiet, whispered conversation, which the boys observed.

To the boys, this seemed unfair. The girls were talking and the teacher didn't say anything. They were supposed to be quiet. So, two of the boys also began to talk. However, it was impossible for these boys to whisper. Soon their deep indistinguishable sounds reached the ear of the teacher, and she turned in the direction of the talking boys and told them in no uncertain terms to leave the auditorium. The boys' response, spoken in disbelief, was "But the girls were talking, too. Why are you sending us out? That's so unfair!"

As the boys sulked, I was reminded that the goodwill of children at this age is not limitless. In this situation these two boys left the auditorium feeling justified in not liking their teacher, who in their mind proved once again that she favored the girls. Some children at this age will quickly latch onto any reason to think that their teacher is unfair because, if they find one, they then feel justified in resisting the more taxing assignments the teacher requires, such as paying attention in class, doing homework carefully, or completing a main lesson book artistically. It may not be a fair or accurate assessment on the part of the students, but it is one of the challenges that many class teachers face.

Fractions

The students in my class ate their lunch together in the classroom, and by fourth grade they could move to a friend's desk and eat together. One day I noticed that a cluster of students up front were talking about some other children in the class. As I listened, I could hear them refer to the other students as "Waldorfian." *Waldorfian* was a derogatory term used to describe certain students in the class who exhibited specific behaviors. They brought their snack in Tupperware containers and ate cut up vegetables like carrots, cauliflower, and broccoli. These students still wore snow pants in winter and didn't know the words of any top-forty songs. The other group, the self-proclaimed "cool kids," brought bags of potato chips or Doritos for snack. They also wore blue jeans to school, even when it snowed. And of course, they knew the words to a number of popular songs, primarily because they had older siblings.

Needless to say, I was concerned. Such divisiveness in a class can be painful, and I needed to speak with the parents to work out how we would address this as a class community. Fortunately, we had a parent meeting coming up, and now I knew what we would speak about. But for me the question was how to present this situation to my parents. This is where the curriculum helped again because what we had with this difficulty was fractions that are introduced in grade four. In the early grades we had been one whole class, but with the nine-year change a greater sense of self-awareness and self-consciousness was being experienced by the students. This awareness made them seek out friends whose interests were similar to theirs. This division caused the whole to break into parts—small groups—and therefore, fractions.

I presented it in this way to the parents, because I wanted them to view this problem as I did, as a situation brought on by a normal stage of child development. I then proposed that what we needed was a common denominator that would enable us to add these fractions back together and recreate the whole. I suggested that our common denominator was that all the children in our class were "Waldorfian" because they all attended the Waldorf school and benefitted from what our school had to offer. The other belief that the parents in my class held in common was inclusiveness. Once we were in accord, and that happened quickly, we could figure out what to do. We decided that we would pay particular attention to the birthday parties and outings outside of school so that children who had been invited in the past were not excluded. The parents also agreed to speak to their children about this matter and to remind them that all of their classmates were their friends. No more needed to be said and the issue was resolved.

It is worth noting that I had confidence that the children in my class were being raised in a healthy manner. Because of this, I could see their behaviors and "misbehaviors" as normal. Children have always been quirky and creative in the ways in which they act out. Viewing my children as healthy enabled me to see behind their behaviors to the developmental changes that were responsible for what I was experiencing whether it was the nine-year change or the twelve-year change. Truthfully every grade has its challenges, and seeing the children in my class as healthy and normal allowed me to say, "It's all good. This is my work and I am glad to do it."

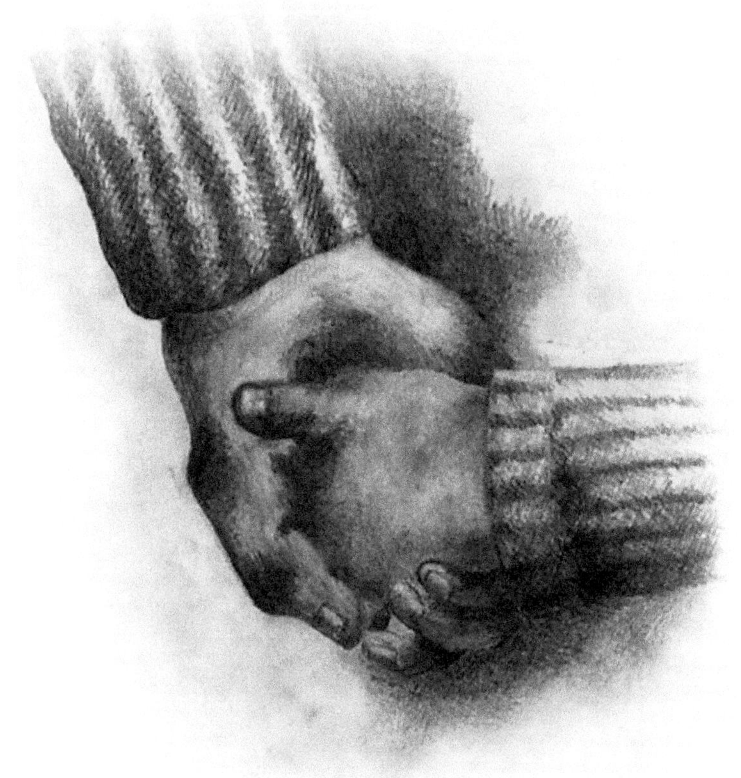

Part Two

The Important Work with Parents

13

Working With Parents

I was convinced after taking two classes from grades one through eight at the Washington Waldorf School that I would not return there to teach. After seventeen years, one of which was spent in the office as an administrator, I went to work for a publishing company—a self-funded sabbatical from teaching. I was ready for a change, and I believed my family was as well.

Next, I set my sights on a Waldorf school in a neighboring state. I had applied there after my teacher training, but was not offered a position. This was now a second chance to work in a beautiful setting at an established school and I was interested. However, on the day of my visit something unexpected happened. I stood in the second-grade classroom at this school and was struck by a strong sense of claustrophobia. The room felt close and it made me uneasy. This was a surprising reaction—one I could not ignore.

Shortly after that visit, I was back at the Washington Waldorf School for parent conferences for my own children. As my wife and I were getting ready to leave, the first-grade teacher invited me into his classroom. He was a new teacher and I was glad to visit. His first-grade room looked lovely, spacious, light-filled, and welcoming, and I thought, "I could teach in this room." This thought stayed with me and caused me to do the unexpected. I applied to take another first grade at the Washington school. It was a significant work decision, one of the best I've made.

I knew some of the mothers who would have children in the class because they were part of a study group that my wife Carol hosted at our house. From a distance, I would hear their discussions on the book *You Are Your Child's First Teacher.* I was struck by the serious manner in which they were taking up the work of parenting, and what I had come to know in my time as a class teacher was that parents play a vital role in a teacher's success in the classroom and when parents and teachers work together for the good of the children, our schools are stronger. I was determined that my new first grade would have a sound parent community, one resting on a relationship of trust and mutual understanding. What I didn't know was how many parents would want their children in this class.

When the number of applicants swelled well beyond the number of children that could fit in the classroom, it turned out that I had to decide which children would be accepted into grade one. But the decision I had to make could not be based on the children. They were all worthy. The parents were the key, and I needed to know if the Waldorf school was really the kind of school they wanted. Over the years I had interviewed parents who were not convinced that the Waldorf approach was the right one for their child. As a school, we would try to "persuade" these parents through workshops, guest speakers, and informal follow-up conversations, but if they remained uncertain, this new relationship would not stand the test of time. These parents would eventually remove their children from the school, and when they left, often after third grade, the other parents would be disappointed and wonder what was wrong with our school that these new friends weren't staying. Yet, what I was sensing was that it had simply taken longer for these parents to realize that the Waldorf school was not the school they were looking for, and that we had avoided speaking about the aspects of our program that might eventually be problematic.

As it happened, I was invited to speak at Acorn Hill, a nearby Waldorf preschool. Because I was going to be the new first grade teacher, many prospective parents were planning to attend the talk. It was important for me to be clear about the work I was hoping to do with this new class and how our school's approach was sound but different.

I chose to focus my talk on a statement that Rudolf Steiner made in his seminal lecture series *The Foundations of Human Experience*. Here is what he said:

> In education we are quite often concerned with the question of separating feeling from willing.... We properly prepare children for later life only when we enable them to successfully separate feeling from willing. Later...they connect their feeling with thinking cognition and, thus, fully meet life.*

I wanted parents to know that separating feeling from willing was essentially about helping grade-school children learn that they can't always do what they feel like doing. And that there are also times when children need to do what they don't feel like doing, such as putting on boots and a raincoat when they go out for recess in inclement weather. I tried to assure the parents that all schools, except maybe free schools, have been doing this for eons. Years ago, Catholic

---

* Steiner, *Rudolf Steiner in the Waldorf School*, p. 123.

schools did this with guilt and a ruler. Military schools did it with pushups and demerits. More mainstream schools have resorted to grades and now rewards, like candy. In the Waldorf school we also do this, but we rely on imagination, repetition, rhythm and the student/teacher relationship. I wanted the parents to know that there would surely be times when I would ask the children to do what they didn't feel like doing.

I waited for questions and there were a number of them. I listened carefully and looked to continue these conversations in the interviews.

It may be worth mentioning that these interviews took place thirty years ago when independent Waldorf schools were not as well known and we were still working to dispel the notion that Waldorf was simply a free and expressive school, one that provided creative, artistic experiences for talented, but somewhat indulged children. Instead, we wanted parents to understand that Waldorf education could serve all children and help them develop a fully human thinking—thinking that would enable them to meet our world with warmth and interest.

I was going to pursue this same issue in a slightly different way when I spoke with the children's kindergarten teachers. How were the children during story time? How were they during circle? Did they play well with their classmates? Would these six-year-old children do what they were asked to do? And, of course: What were the parents like? Answers to these questions would help to shape my conversations with the parents.

Before these meetings, I had an important request that I directed to the spiritual world. It went something like this:

"You know me, and you know that I can miss what I need to see. Please help me to notice what I should." This was the prayer that I carried into my interviews, one that I believe helped me to be more awake and receptive. Yet, even with this help, I still could misjudge a situation.

We received an application for a child who was not in our kindergarten but who had a sister in our older grades. During the interview I asked a couple of questions to get a sense of what the boy was like. The first was, "What does your son like to do at home?" Their answer, which was candid and honest, was, "Not much. He likes to sit on the couch and watch television." There is usually no wrong answer to this question, but in a Waldorf interview this was one. A little later in the conversation, after I had a clearer sense of the boy's phlegmatic nature, I asked what foods he liked to eat. "Oh, he only eats sweets. He won't eat vegetables." "What responsibilities does he have at home?" "Oh, he doesn't like to help around the house." I left the meeting thinking that this child was allowed to do whatever he liked and that the parents were not trying to understand our school's approach. My decision seemed clear. I did not accept the student into the first grade.

The boy's parents were upset but it was their response (after they wrote a letter to the board) that got my attention. Whenever the mom or dad came to the school with their son to pick up his sister, they had him come to the first-grade room and greet me, which he did with a warm smile and a handshake. After a few of these sweet and sincere encounters, it became clear to me that their child should be in our class. And when there was an opening for second grade, we reached out to the family and he was enrolled.

In eighth grade, when the class was graduating, I was surprised to remember that this fellow had not been part of the class from grade one. He was clearly such an integral part of our group. It was as if he had always been with us. He was a pleasure to teach, and his parents were truly supportive. I should also mention that this student became a vegan chef, an avid reader, and he sang beautifully in community choral groups—just another reminder of how much I needed to learn.

From the beginning of first grade, I was determined to take up the work with my new class parents as seriously as I took up the work with their children. However, I did not imagine that my assignment was to tell the parents how to raise their children, but rather to convey to them in a clear and lively manner the ideas at the heart of our Waldorf education. They had chosen this school, and I wanted to encourage them to embrace these ideas at home.

A good example of this had to do with screen time. I understood that screen time in the home could be a complicated issue, one that could be strongly influenced by the age of the other siblings. In a family with a first grader and, say, a seventh- or eighth-grade student, it can be difficult to have no screen exposure. It was that way in our home when our daughter grew up with two teenage brothers. It was not impossible for her to come inside on a late weekend afternoon and see them watching a sporting event. I remember a particular time when she sat down on the couch and I heard her ask her brothers why there was a blue devil on the television. It was during the NCAA March Madness basketball tournament and Duke was playing.

I figured if this happened in our family and we were committed to no screen time for young children, it could happen in other families as well. Could I really ask parents to refrain completely? Instead, I spoke with the parents at a first-grade meeting about why they had chosen Waldorf education and how they wanted their children in a dynamic learning environment, one that fostered active, hands-on involvement in the learning process. I went on to say that if we value active participation, why would we let our young children watch television when studies show that metabolism rates during television viewing are comparable to times when we are sleeping. No parent disputed this research. We all knew exactly how we felt when we "vegged out" in front of the TV after a hard day at work.

I could simply say, "We all agree that purposeful activity is good for children. I am counting on you to support the education you are making great sacrifices to offer your children." The parents in my new class responded well to this conversation.

I valued our parent meetings because they provided an important time to speak together about the principles and practices of Waldorf education. I knew that when these meetings were held, I hoped for full parent participation. For that reason, I never planned more than three parent meetings a year. I knew teachers who had a parent meeting nearly every month, but I also knew that those meetings were attended by about half the parents. I wanted every child represented so that if we spoke about an important topic, all the families were informed. I always sent a notice home several weeks before the meeting so the parents could put the date on their calendars, and then a reminder when the date drew near.

But the last reminder came from the children. After they had cleaned their desks and set out their work, they crafted a handwritten invitation that went home in the lunch box. I was counting on my persuasive students to say something about the meeting to their parents.

I was also extremely protective of our meeting time. I planned a clear and concise agenda with a definite starting and ending time. There were about fifteen minutes to socialize and look at the children's work before the start of the meeting, and then our conversation went for an hour, not more. My parents were busy and I valued their willingness to attend our meetings. I wouldn't squander our time together. And when a difficult question was asked five minutes before the end of the parent meeting, which often seemed to be the case, I knew I could not do justice to that question in a short time. I either took that question up at a later date or met with that parent individually, rather than extend the meeting.

There were many topics we would consider in these parent meetings. Often, they were the more elusive aspects of Waldorf education. These are extremely important, challenging topics because they are often based on a spiritual view of the child, and spiritual understandings are often counter-cultural and nuanced. An example of this is the way that the Waldorf school teaches reading. It is essential that teachers find a way to explain our approach so that we gain the parents' confidence through their understanding, not just through a leap of faith because the teacher believes this strongly, or because Rudolf Steiner said so. As teachers, we get only so many of those "leaps of faith," and we shouldn't use them all up in the early grades.

In his lecture series *Awakening to Community*, Rudolf Steiner said, "It is just in presenting anthroposophy that every attempt should be made to portray what has thus been raised to a clear, conscious level in all its elemental aliveness, to offer it in so living a form that it seems like people's own naïve experiencing and feeling. We must make sure that we do this."*

Explaining how we teach reading requires an imaginative, thoughtful explanation so that our parents can share our understanding. When I speak with parents about reading, I invariably ask them to think about what they have seen around our city, Washington, D.C. Our downtown is marked by dozens of construction cranes. These large, steel structures stand over deeply excavated foundations. What we all know is that the deeper the foundation, the longer it will take before we see signs of progress above ground. But what we also know is that the deeper the foundation, the taller and more substantial the future structure will be.

I want our parents to understand that in first grade we are creating a deep foundation of literacy. We are teaching our children to read in a multidimensional way. We will engage them visually and research shows that the part of the brain where letter recognition occurs is the same part of the brain where reading occurs.** We will also engage the students auditorily through stories, poems, songs, and tongue-twisters, deepening their phonemic awareness. We will involve them kinesthetically through movement, modelling, and painting. This is the rich, multidimensional foundation of reading instruction that is part of the Waldorf

---

*   Steiner, *Awakening to Community*, p. 92
** Konnikova, "What's Lost when Handwriting Fades," *The New York Times*, June 2, 2014.

student's first grade experience. Most of this beginning work occurs below ground level and provides the solid foundation upon which a child's reading ability will develop in the years to come. I will never say that we don't teach reading in a Waldorf school. We just do it differently.

America does not just have a problem with illiteracy; we have an "a-literacy" problem as well. There are millions of children who can read, but don't. Our goal at a Waldorf school is to teach children to read through active participation, to be moved emotionally by what they read, as well as to enjoy to learn through reading. We want them to become lifelong readers. This is what we are trying to put in place. Strong, substantial structures like this simply take longer.

Waldorf Education is moving against the educational current, and rightfully so. We are committed to an education that develops the full humanity of our students in an unfortunately dehumanizing time. Because our approach is markedly different, our parents will need repeated reassurance. Our parents are aware of our dedication to Waldorf education and to the writings of Rudolf Steiner. If they have a worry, however, it is that our approach is too narrow and insulated. We also need to open our awareness to what is being considered outside of Waldorf and reassure our parents that we are part of a larger educational conversation. This will help to create the trust that will enable us to work together for the wellbeing of the children.

14

Hold Them Close and Let Them Go

I learn my parenting lessons in the oddest ways but, even so, this last lesson took me by surprise. I was trying to engage my fifteen-year-old daughter in cheerful dinner conversation, refraining from serious questions about homework or music practice. And I thought I had succeeded when my jokes elicited a chuckle. But the joy was short-lived. She looked up from her plate, lowered her fork and said, "Dad, you are like so bipolar." My smile froze and she left me wondering if this parenting roller coaster we were on with its dramatic ups and downs had left a permanent mark on my psyche. How could it not? Parenting is awash in bipolar opposites— highs and lows, joys and sorrows, work and play, responsibility and freedom. The list is endless and that's what makes parenting such an emotional stretch. I wanted to reply, "Of course I'm bipolar. I'm a parent."

Parenting is an art and like all of the arts it exists between opposites. Artists always work with polarities: light and dark, space and counter-space, foreground and background, piano and forte. The only difference with parenting is that we don't get to practice our art in solitude. We're not at a piano in the quiet confines of a studio, or in a lovely pastoral setting with watercolors and an easel. Instead, we get to fashion our artwork in the carpool or in the kitchen, and always at the dinner table. Our creative endeavors take place seven days a week, at all hours of the day, and over long stretches of time. And because parenting is a most demanding art, it requires even more conscious awareness to reconcile and mediate opposites. That is what makes it so complicated.

The Parenting Essentials

Parenting doesn't seem complicated when we start out on the journey. Aside from loving our children, there are essentially two basic assignments: provide for our children and protect them. These are the primary parenting responsibilities that we take up selflessly in order to build a foundation of trust, safety, and dependability. It is the important work that we do on a number of levels. We provide nourishing food and clean clothes for our children, but more than this we establish a consistent routine of caring. We hold our children when they cry, change them when they're wet, talk to them, sing to them, wash them, and comfort them continually. Amidst the confusion of the first weeks of a child's life, we establish a dependable rhythm of consistent care. This protective environment enables our children to rest assured and to begin their lives in a healthy way. In their book *The Irreducible Needs of Childhood*, T. Berry Brazleton and Stanley Greenspan note that having a safe, predictable environment is one of childhood's irreducible needs, because it influences the way that children's nervous systems develop. Calm, dependable environments give rise to calm, dependable children.*

A protected physical environment must also be accompanied by a protected emotional environment. The softness of our words, the gentleness of our touch, our patient attention,

---

* Brazelton and Greenspan, *The Irreducible Needs of Children*, p. 57.

all convey to our children another level of safety. In the home, feelings are safeguarded as well. But the confusing part of the parenting paradox is that protection as a parenting goal is inherently flawed. Years ago a friend of mine went to a marriage counselor. She was told that in relationships, the very characteristic that draws us to an individual, will in the end repel us. Find a reliable, dependable spouse and their predictability will eventually disappoint us. Become involved with a carefree, free-spirited person and sooner or later we will long for steadiness and responsibility. Ralph Waldo Emerson's words probably express this best: "Every excess causes a defect.... Every sweet hath its sour." The same is true with parenting. Provide the important protective environment for our children and over time the need to provide a markedly different environment will make itself known. The pendulum invariably swings the other way.

Overprotecting Our Children

Currently, in our society we are much better at protecting our children than we are at allowing them to develop independence and a little daring. With all of the best intentions we have sequestered our children in our homes. Fear of automobiles, pedophiles, injuries, and lawsuits has denied our children the opportunities we had growing up. We roller-skated without knee pads and helmets, walked to school, to our friends' houses, and to stores without supervision. We played in the schoolyard, climbed trees and fences, and stayed out after dark. So few children do the same today.

In her book *The Blessing of a Skinned Knee: Using Jewish Traditions to Raise Self-reliant Children*, Wendy Mogel notes that it is also a parent's job to teach children to manage risks. Mogel contends that if people today were faced with the opportunity to do something dramatic and life-changing, like the Exodus from Egypt, most would decline, enslaved more by fear than by Pharaoh.*

During the second half of childhood, parents need to help children manage risks as a counter balance to the protective home environment we have developed during their early years.

For ten years my wife and I worked at a summer institute in Maine. This was a fine arrangement for our family as it allowed us to leave the heat and humidity of Washington, D.C., in the summer and to spend six weeks in northern New England. From the time our daughter was four, we all headed north in July, and our daughter took part in the program that was provided for the children. In many ways the environment there was ideal. The Rudolf Steiner Institute was housed on a small college campus and my daughter and her summer friends could walk anywhere without restriction.

Just prior to her fourteenth birthday, our daughter began voicing reservations about returning to Maine. She complained that there was nothing to do. We reminded her that there were art classes, kayaking trips, beach excursions, swimming, innumerable opportunities provided by the program, but she was adamant. So, we began to explore other options. My wife did some research to find alternatives and discovered a wilderness canoe trip solely for teenage girls led by young women guides. This trip would be vigorous and rugged. The group would head off for a ten-day adventure with extensive paddling and extended portages. They would

---

*   Mogel, *The Blessing of a Skinned Knee,* p. 89.

have to camp out, cook their own food, make do without the comforts of home (no showers, no toilets), and be at the mercy of the bugs and the weather. We thought for sure that our daughter would express no interest whatsoever. We were wrong. She wanted to go.

Sending her on this trip was a huge step for us. We had to leave her with her brother in Boston and know that she was getting on a plane for Canada and that, when she got off, one of the tour leaders, whom we had never met, would be there to meet her and a few other girls and take them six hours north of Toronto to the base camp, where they would join the group to begin their trip. The only communication that we would have during the two weeks she was away was a phone message that she had arrived in Toronto safely and two email messages—one when they left the basecamp for their canoe trip and one when they returned.

At the end of the two weeks, my wife and I drove back to Boston eager to pick her up at the airport. When she came through customs with the flight attendant (she flew as an unaccompanied minor), we were there waiting. She looked so pleased with herself, self-confident and mature. She was strong from the canoeing and portaging, healthy from the days outdoors and different, not just because of the hair rinse that the girls had shared on their adventure, but also because she had been through a rite of passage and was so pleased with herself.

The next year, she was eager to return. She saved her babysitting money and spent nineteen days in the wilderness braving mosquitoes, whitewater, and the SARS epidemic. Protecting our children is essential, but not protecting them can be just as important.

Parents as Providers

Providing for our children is another of parenting's paradoxes. Because our children start out in life depending on us for everything, it is vital that we live fully into our role as providers. Food, clothing, and meaningful experiences are all a part of what parents work hard to provide. The more thought and care we put into providing for our children at an early age, the more they benefit. Providing healthy food, warm clothing, and good medical care are just the kind of assignments that good parents take seriously. It is our job to provide the very best for our children, and over time these decisions will involve schools, camps, after-school lessons, and all sorts of teams. But here too, Emerson's words apply: "Every excess has its defect.... Every sweet hath its sour."

In his book *Too Much of a Good Thing: Raising Children of Character in an Indulgent Age,* Dan Kindlon points out that providing too much for our children for too long, impedes character development. When Kindlon did a survey on "too good to be true teenagers," the kinds of healthy children parents hope to raise, he found that there were certain characteristics that these young people had in common. They cleaned their own rooms. They did not have a phone in their room (I assume that also means a cell phone). And they did some kind of community service.[*] What the parents provided was very simple—these children ate dinner regularly as a family.

What is clear from this study is that we should always provide our children with opportunities to give as well as receive. This can mean different things in different

---

[*] Kindlon, *Too Much of a Good Thing,* p. 177.

families. It can mean that children make their own beds or do the dishes. It can mean that adolescents do their own laundry or clean the bathroom. And with teenagers, it can mean that they work outside of the home on weekends or in the summer to earn their own spending money, keeping in mind that independence fosters responsibility, and that leads to self-esteem.

A number of years ago, the state of California offered a work program for young people modeled after the Civilian Conservation Corps, the federally funded program during the Depression. The California program promised "hard work, long hours, and low pay." It had a waiting list, mostly with young people from well-to-do families who wanted to find out what they were really worth.

In the end, children must provide for themselves. How many kids today pay for their own car insurance, their gasoline, their cell phones, or their credit card bills in college? What message do we send our children when we give them so much, other than the message of privilege or entitlement?

Parenting has to be a bipolar undertaking. We are called on to protect our children, not over-protect them, to provide for them, not indulge them. These are the challenges that parenting sets before us; as with any art form, there are no easy answers. We simply have to be present in the moment and move between the opposites to achieve the right balance. Sometimes this work seems overwhelming, and I must say there are nights when I get down. It is then that I look for a little help with this work and this quotation by E. F. Schumacher from *Small is Beautiful* helps:

> Through all our lives we are faced with the task of reconciling opposites that, in logical thought, cannot be

reconciled.... How can one reconcile the demands of freedom and discipline in education? Countless mothers and teachers, in fact, do it, but no one can write down a solution. They do it by bringing into the situation a force that belongs to a higher level where opposites are transcended—the power of love.*

These words remind me that I am just a struggling artist who really loves his work.

---

* Schumacher, *Small Is Beautiful,* pp. 97, 98.

15

What the Fathers Taught Me about Parenting

I never imagined that I would work with parents other than the parents of the children in my class. It happened unexpectedly. Our school had a Wednesday-morning study group, and during one gathering the conversation shifted from education to parenting, and eventually to the parenting of the fathers. I don't know what was said about the dads, but I am sure it was not all complimentary. The mothers who were there that morning thought it would be a good idea to have a talk at the school for these men. Because I was a teacher and a father, I was a likely candidate, and I was asked to speak and gladly accepted. I had often felt that our school needed to build a bridge to the dads to involve them more fully in the school. The title of my talk was, "The Challenges of Being a Waldorf Father," and fifty men came out that evening.

Afterward, one of the dads approached me and said, "This is great. Can't we continue to meet?" So, we started a Fathers' Group at our school, and about twenty men attended regularly. The conversations we had were wideranging. We spoke about Waldorf education and about the challenges and joys of parenting. But the rich conversations, which I never anticipated, were about our experiences as sons and how we were parented.

As the facilitator of our group, I felt that it was my responsibility to come prepared with a question that would encourage our conversation. One day I was lucky enough to hit upon a surprisingly good question: "What is the best memory that you have of your father?" I wanted the men to relate these memories vividly so that we could see what those moments were like. I also ended up asking them what age they were when the memory occurred.

As I listened to the fathers, I was amazed. The men were presenting wonderful examples of what it means to be a good father. But the biggest surprise occurred when I realized that the very principles that were central to good Waldorf teaching were also at the heart of good parenting. Good dads continually engage their children in a three-dimensional way—actively, emotionally, and thoughtfully. And this threefold engagement was most effective when the needed emphasis corresponded with one of the three stages of child development—active in the first seven years, emotionally engaged in the second seven years, and thoughtfully involved in the teenage years. The traditional Waldorf "head, heart, and hands" paradigm provided a practical guideline for establishing meaningful and satisfying parenting in the home.

The Young Child

Whenever we speak about parenting and the young child, we must remember that in the first phase of childhood, we are creating a foundation of guidance. This provides the gentle footing for helping our children learn the important practices that are part of family life. These are the continually occurring activities in which children need to take part. Without forethought these activities can become problematic. Mealtime, bedtime, breakfast, carpool—all of these have their challenges.

During one of our fathers' groups, one of the dads asked, with a note of disbelief, how a preschool teacher can simply start to sing a certain song and the children immediately know that it is time to clean up the toys with which they were playing. "Miracles" like this don't just happen. They are the result of the consistent repetition of an activity, one that recurs gently, but at the same time rhythmically, each day. This routine is based on a teacher's firmly held intention. When we approach young children at clean-up time, the important word is *"we." "We* are going to clean up now."

The teacher begins the song and joins the children in this activity, modeling how to put the toys on the shelf and the pieces of wood and stones into the baskets. But the teacher is also checking to see that all of the children are taking part, and if a child isn't participating, the teacher will walk closer to that child and invite them to join the others. until the cleanup is complete. When this routine occurs consistently, rhythmically, the habit of cleaning up will be established. In a classroom it may take all of September and part of October for the habit to be fully established, but eventually it will happen that the teacher starts to sing a certain song and the children begin to put their toys away.

The same approach will work in the home. The main difference is that for a parent this usually occurs after a long day of work. To have the wherewithal to involve ourselves in this way, to clean up with our child, to see that they are helping, and that the toys and books, the crayons and paper, are going back where they belong, requires something extra, something we draw on for the good of our children. Truly it is easier and faster to clean things up by ourselves. But helping our children develop a sense of responsibility through their participation is far more important. The same is true when children help to set the table and to clear their place after dinner or to put their clothes away at bedtime.

I often ask parents to think about their friends who don't have children and to imagine what their friends' lives are like on Sundays. How natural it is for them to sleep until 8:30, have a leisurely cup of coffee, and then to spend time reading a book or the paper. They might even go out for brunch and have an uninterrupted adult conversation. Yet, I am quick to remind parents that they have chosen a nobler path. They are on a journey toward sainthood for as they raise their children, they will develop a range of really fine qualities such as patience, selflessness, love, empathy, perseverance, and more. It is true, parenting requires considerable effort, but it will reshape us in remarkable ways.

It is hard work to raise children, and young children are particularly labor-intensive. But the young child offers us help. First, children love repetition and routine. That is why they often want the same story each evening, and if you change a sentence or skip a word, they will let you know. Also, our children love us so deeply that they watch us continually and learn just by observing and imitating our actions. This powerful inclination to imitate is central to the way in which the young child learns. If there is something that we want our children to do, such as put their shoes in a special place or put the cap back on the toothpaste tube, we simply need to consciously provide a model by doing this in our child's presence each and every day. Eventually they will do it, too. And just like the preschool teacher who consciously repeats the cleanup routine, it is really the adult's self-discipline that is central in helping our children learn.

The Grade-School Child: Our Emotional Connection

As our children enter the second phase of childhood, around the age of six or seven, we can see changes beginning to occur. Their arms and legs lengthen; their faces grow thinner as "baby fat" disappears, and their baby teeth start to fall out. But not all the changes are physical. Some occur on an inner level with a noticeable deepening of feeling. I have often felt that children love their friends at this age in a way that is unequaled later in life. They also have the same deep affection for their family, their grandparents, cousins, aunts, and uncles, and for their pets. This abundance of feeling is a marked characteristic of the grade-school years.

When the fathers that I worked with shared memories that came from this second phase of childhood, they were noticeably different from the ones that came from an earlier age. They were no longer simply memories of what their fathers did—working with tools around the house or in the garage—but now they were memories with an added dimension, one connected to feelings.

One man recalled how his father would come home after work and put on classical music. As the LP played loudly on the stereo, his father conducted an imagined orchestra. He would wave his arms and move his head so that his hair would shake. His son could see that his father, who was a decidedly reserved man, was completely engaged in that moment, absorbed in the music he loved.

Another memory was of a father who somehow managed to pack an entire family—his wife, five children, a friend, a grandmother, and an aunt—into a station wagon, along with enough food and clothing for a weeklong annual trip to the Jersey Shore. As he drove on a warm summer morning, with his left arm resting on the open driver side window, he would sing. His children noticed.

We know that a child's feeling life is pronounced at this age, but what we don't always realize is that children pay considerable attention to what their parents feel. Our children are connected to us in mysterious ways, and parents' feelings will be an essential part of their children's experience.

A parent's emotional life creates the "weather" in the home. We want that climate to be temperate, not stormy or icy. One way to assist with this is to be at our best. One of the memories I heard from a father's group that I facilitated in the Midwest was of a dad who would go into his son's room on a Saturday morning and wake him by wrestling with him in bed. And the boy would think, "My dad is home *all* day." This memory always helps me to remember how long all day was when I was a child. Time should be an expansive, heartfelt experience for children.

Our use of time can deepen our emotional connection with our children. The events that recur regularly, like an annual trip to the beach, the summer camping adventure, or an often-repeated hike or bike ride that ends with a stop at a favorite ice cream shop, create lasting emotional memories. In addition, our celebration of holidays and birthdays, when they become part of a family ritual, become valued traditions.

One of the most priceless memories that I heard was from a Canadian fellow who all through his childhood played hockey. His father would take him to his practices and his games. During the games, his father would stand with the other parents up in the balcony above the rink, always in the same place just above the goal. Sadly, this young man's father died when he was in high school, and in a hockey game shortly after his father's death he scored three goals. After the last goal, he skated away from the net wishing that his father was still around to witness his hat trick. Just then he happened to look up to the balcony, to the very spot where his father always stood, and there was an open space with parents crowded together on both sides. It was as if space had been left for his dad, and he felt that his father was still showing up to watch him play. So much of what we are asked to do with our children is simply to show up, care deeply, and be an integral part of their lives.

Discipline Situations are Inevitable

Time is also important when we have the inevitable disciplinary encounters with our children. As with teachers, parents do better in challenging moments if they have ample time. However, parents today are often unfairly stressed, given the hectic pace of modern life with continual texts, phone calls, emails, and unexpected traffic delays. When our schedule runs late, it noticeably affects our family life. And when dinner is late, our children can have low blood sugar, and arguments occur. If dinner's been late, bedtime is usually late as well, and tired children can lack the wherewithal to get ready for bed without procrastinating. Somewhere on this continuum, a parent's intervention will be needed, but if that intervention leads to an unpleasant emotional interaction, everyone goes to bed feeling badly.

More Dramatic Changes

As a class teacher, I am continually awed by how much my students changed over the course of eight years. The vast difference between first graders and eighth graders is astounding. What I also noticed was that, aside from the steady growth and maturity that took place each year, there were pronounced inner changes that occurred in formidable spurts. At these times, the developmental journey seemed to pick up speed as a young person's sense of self and independence increased.

This increase in independence is exactly what we hope for in our children. And yet at each of these times of change our parenting can be called into question. Not only will the habits that we have worked so diligently to set in place be tested, but bigger issues such as respect, trustworthiness, and truthfulness can be undermined as well.

This certainly happened with one of our sons. When he was around ten years old, he developed a fascination with four-letter words. If we reminded him to clear his place after dinner or to practice his viola, he would answer, "FINE." And if he was asked to dry the dishes or put his backpack in his room, his reply would be, "SURE." Each of his responses was said with a strong measure of annoyance that felt confrontational.

Eventually, we sat him down for a chat. We spoke about his good qualities, how many people liked him and thought he was lively, humorous, thoughtful and talented. Then we told him that we were worried that strangers weren't going to see his good qualities if he responded to requests in a rude manner. So we decided to help him. I made a small card and lettered it in calligraphy. It said, "No Dessert." We told him that, if he answered in a rude manner, we would simply put the card on the refrigerator, and the next time we had dessert he wouldn't get any. His response: "Fine."

We didn't have to wait long before the "no dessert" card made its way to the refrigerator, and that night when we had ice cream for dessert, there were three bowls on the table, not four. Our son looked up and said, "You meant it?"

A number of years ago, I had a radio show called "On Parenting" in Washington, D.C., on Pacifica Radio. One of my guests was Kim Payne, a noted author and parent educator. Kim was on to speak about discipline. One of the callers phoned in to say that when he was a boy and did something inappropriate, he would get "whooped" by his father. He wanted to know what Kim thought about corporal punishment. In his inimitable way, Kim told a story about how he would misbehave when he was a boy and how there would be times when his mother would get upset with him. When she reprimanded him, she would get a look on her face that let Kim know that she meant it. "That's the important thing with our children and discipline," Kim said. "We have to mean it."

As parents, we are called on to combine our love for our children with firmness. This is not always easy, but it is necessary. Recently, I was involved in creating a workshop for fathers with a Native elder and artist, Stan Padilla. As one part of our weekend work, Stan Padilla was planning to whittle with the men. He wanted the fathers to have the experience of carving with oak and with willow. He believed that these two very different woods would help men understand the importance of blending opposites in fathering. The oak, for the Native people, is connected with fire. It is a strong wood, the kind of strength that engenders upright-ness, dependability, and dignity—essential characteristics for fathers. The willow, on the other hand, relates to the element of water. It is a gentler wood—fluid, flexible, supple—equally important qualities for a dad. Embracing this paradox is the essence of parenting today. Whenever I sit with young dads and ask them what qualities they want to bring to their parenting, these contrasting characteristics found in the oak and in the willow are mentioned.

The Teenage Years: Communication Matters

The way that we parent will be influenced by the way we were parented as children. We will either have been given parenting models to emulate or we will have marked ideas of how we want to do things differently. Because my father and I were not able to speak openly together, I had a continual worry that I would not be able to converse freely with my own children when they became teenagers. I repeatedly found that the remarks I made seemed to put an end to a conversation rather than enabling it to grow.

It is just when communication is of the greatest importance that it can become the most challenging. Finding successful ways to speak with a teenager requires careful attention to those times when young people talk more freely. Some teenagers prefer to talk late at night and some talk more when they eat side-by-side rather than face-to-face. It can be different for each child. And sometimes conversations just show up in a surprising way.

When my daughter was in high school, she and I needed to drive from our home near Washington, D.C., to New York to pick her mother up at a conference. It was an early summer evening and we stopped at a rest stop for food. Unfortunately, there were tour buses at the rest stop and the food court was packed. So we ordered lattes at the Starbucks and got back in the car. A few minutes later my daughter became uncharacteristically chatty and began to tell me what she was thinking about college and what she wanted to do with her life. I was so amazed and grateful to hear her open up like this. Then I realized that in the busy-ness of the food court I had forgotten to order her a *decaf* latte. I just smiled and listened.

More important than the timing and location is the way in which we listen to our teenagers. Our ability to hear what they say without judgment, to refrain from giving advice, especially to abstain from asking questions that are really advice in disguise ("Have you thought of dating other people?") can make all the difference. Young people are so sensitive that they can detect judgment in our expression and our tone of voice, and anytime they feel judged, they withdraw. But if we ask them what they think and listen with genuine interest, it allows them to speak freely. Deep listening can help wick up a young person's unspoken thoughts into words and enable them to voice ideas that were previously not fully formed. At those moments we are both learning.

We are going to need to have many important conversations with our teenagers, and they won't always be easy. Because they are developing their critical thinking skills, they will question us repeatedly. These conversations can be taxing. Teenagers are learning how to think and how to know their own minds. We should always be interested in what they have to say, but understand that they don't often

want to hear what we think. And this is just as it should be
if they are going to learn to think for themselves.

The environmental author Scott Russell Sanders wrote
an intriguing book entitled *Hunting for Hope: A Father's
Journey*. In his book, Sanders writes about the difficulties
he was having with his son, how they would argue repeatedly about soccer and the use of the car. But he sensed that
the problems went deeper than that, so he agreed to go on
a backpacking trip with his son in the high country in the
Rockies. But the trip did not go as Sanders had imagined.

Toward the end of a long day's hike, his son Jesse wanted
to press on and set their tent above the snow line and camp
at Thunder Lake around 11,000 feet.

"We're not equipped for the snow," the father replied.

"Sure we are. Why do you think I bought a new
sleeping bag? Why did I call ahead and reserve snow-
shoes?... I can't believe you're wimping out on me, Dad.
All you want to do is poke around in the foothills."

Sanders spoke back, "This isn't wild enough for
you? What do you need—avalanches, grizzlies?"

As it happened at that moment hikers came around
the bend. Two elderly people with three small children
in tow, all carrying canteens and little backpacks. When
they passed, Jesse spoke.

"We're in the wilds, huh Dad? That's why the trail is
full of grandparents and kids."

Jesse walked away angrily, but his father called out
to him, "Is this how it's going to be? You're going to
spoil the trip because I won't camp on the snow?"

Jesse turned and glared, "You're the one spoil-
ing the trip. You and your hang-ups. You always ruin
everything!"

When they eventually returned to the car the next day, Sanders turned to his son and said, "How do I ruin everything?'

[His son replied,] "You wouldn't understand. You're just so out of touch with my whole world. You hate everything that's fun. You hate television and movies and video games."

"You hate advertising," he said quickly, rolling now.

"You hate billboards and developers and logging companies and big corporations. You hate snowmobiles and jet skis.... You look at any car and all you think is pollution. You say fast food is poisoning our bodies. You think business is a conspiracy to rape the earth."

Sanders responded, "None of that bothers you?"

"Of course it does. But that's the world. That's where we've got to live.... What's the good of spitting on it?"

"I don't spit on it."

"You do. Maybe not with your mouth, but with your eyes. Your view is totally dark. It bums me out.... There's no room for hope. I have to believe there's a way out of this mess. Otherwise, what's the point. Why study, why work—why do anything if it's all going to hell?"*

How we are inwardly when we meet our children makes all the difference. These words from a small pamphlet entitled, "Reflections on Discipline" express this so well.

The adolescent looks you in the eye fleetingly. If the you he sees is either too pedantic or too personal, he is alienated. He will turn away. (He would rather you look through him than at him.) But if he sees in you a modest common sense, humor, some rapport with and success in the objective world—and over all a sense for

---

*   Sanders, *Hunting for Hope,* pp. 6–9.

what stands higher than you, higher than himself—he secretly rejoices. His eyes will seek out yours again.*

Parenting is such a long journey, and it will repeatedly ask for our best. We are not supposed to be perfect, but we are asked to learn continuously through each of the three phases of childhood. A large part of that learning will involve getting to know ourselves and our shortcomings. Our children will regularly point these out. Keep in mind that it is usually the child who is most like us that will do this with particular ease. You can call this "fate" or "karma" or attribute it to DNA, but if we pay attention to our shortcomings, try not to make the same mistake twice, and work earnestly to improve, we will all benefit. Parents give a remarkable gift whenever they are able to change themselves out of the love they have for their children.

---

* Gardner, "Reflections on Discipline," p. 12.

16

The Spiritual and Religious Needs of Children

And in the night the heavy earth is falling,
From darkness into loneliness we are falling,
But there is one whose hands hold that falling
endlessly, gently.   —Rilke

Whenever I am asked what children are like today and if I have noticed any changes over the forty-five years that I've been a teacher, people hear me say that the children today are like *sons/suns*. Those hearing me say this immediately ask if I teach only boys. "No," I reply, "I teach SUNS, children who think that they are the center of the universe and that everything revolves around them." Learning to defer to another, to put yourself second, and to truly listen to others are capacities that can now take years to develop.

Another characteristic that I now find in children is anxiety. Children today are noticeably more apprehensive, fearful, and worried than in the past. It is hard to pinpoint the cause. Currently, much has to do with the pandemic, but it could also be the aftermath of 9/11 and the numerous security checkpoints that have become the new normal. Or perhaps it is due to the wanton acts of violence in our country and abroad, actions that dominate the nightly news and the front pages of our newspapers. Children need a countering influence to the unsettling fear engendered by these events and the conversations they incite. Young people need to feel held by something greater than themselves.

This spiritual awareness that the poet Rilke describes, that we are held by an ineffable force, sustained Abraham Lincoln and Martin Luther King Jr. in difficult times. It can also sustain and comfort our children. And yet, fewer and fewer parents offer their children an experience of spiritual and religious life.

Children have an authentic spiritual awareness, and it is often quite developed even at a young age. One example that comes to mind is told by Sir Ken Robinson in his excellent TED talk on "Creativity in Education." He relates the story of a kindergarten student who is busy drawing as her teacher approaches. When the teacher asks her what she is drawing, the little girl replies, "I'm drawing God." The teacher, unsettled by this remark, responds, "But nobody knows what God looks like." The young girl looks up and replies, "They will in a minute."

This kind of spiritual certainty lives in children.*

I often ask adults if they had meaningful spiritual or religious experiences when they were children. I know I had them and I was an unlikely candidate as I spent most of my childhood in a New York City school yard playing just about anything with a ball. But when I look back at the meaningful moments in my early years, I come to the conclusion that my spiritual and religious awareness was as developed as my understanding of sports.

Recently I moderated a panel discussion with individuals of different faiths, and I asked them about their childhood

____

* Sir Ken Robinson, https://youtu.be/17Ye368aQVk.

religious experiences. One man, whose grandfather was a cantor, spoke about Shabbat and the deep peace that accompanied that time, and how much he valued those Friday evening visits to his grandfather's house. His remarks reminded me of this poem by Marcia Falk.

> Three generations back
> my family had only
> to light a candle
> and the world parted.
> Today, Friday afternoon,
> I disconnect clocks and phones.
> When night fills my house
> with passages,
> I begin saving
> my life.*

Another panelist spoke about being raised in the Hindu tradition and how excited she was when her family or a friend's family would open the doors of a small closet in their home to reveal an altar to the God Ganesh. These experiences were culturally important to a family that had emigrated from India, but they offered her much more than that.

A woman, who is now a priest, spoke of a night when she woke up from an unsettling dream and made her way to her parents' room. When she opened the door, she saw her father, the much-respected town veterinarian, on his knees praying beside the bed. She said that until that moment it had never occurred to her that adults prayed. Her parents always said prayers with the children, but seeing her father pray was profoundly moving.

---

* Muller, "Sabbath," p. 21.

Similarly, a Muslim woman told of a little room that had been built just off the kitchen in her grandparents' house. It was a small, private space for the daily devotional prayers. One day she said that the door was open slightly, and she saw her grandmother praying with her white prayer shawl over her head and felt that her grandmother looked like a heavenly apparition.

Childhood experiences are formative if adults don't "talk them away." In the movie *Before Sunrise,* there is a scene in which Ethan Hawke's character is relating a childhood memory to a young Julie Delpy. He speaks of a time when he was about six years old, a time shortly after his grandmother's death. He was standing in his backyard, having just learned how to hold his thumb over the end of the garden hose to make a fine spray of water. He was aiming the hose in the direction of the sun when he saw his grandmother standing behind the rainbow that appeared in the mist, smiling at him lovingly. He kept spraying the water for a good while, and then he took his finger off the hose. The rainbow vanished and so did his grandmother.

Ethan Hawke said that when he went inside to tell his parents what had occurred, they sat him down and explained to him that when someone dies they're gone, and no matter how much we love them they won't be with us anymore. Ethan Hawke's comment: "But I knew what I saw."

We need to protect and respect our children's spiritual awareness and nurture it as it changes as they grow older. This spiritual awareness will eventually be concealed and hidden from us, but it is not gone.

As parents we also need to be aware that under the surface of our children's day to day lives there is a stream of spiritual awareness, and that children need experiences that touch that awareness. A good way to stay connected with this is through the understandings of the Indigenous people of our country. Spiritual insights have always permeated the Native people's consciousness. These understandings were often much more profound than those of the missionaries who tried to convert them, as is evidenced in the following story related by Ernest Thompson Seton.

> Many years ago in Montana, I heard a missionary severely rebuke an Indian for driving a team of horses on Sunday. The Indian looked puzzled. He was merely minding his business and caring for his work and family. The missionary reiterated that this was the Lord's Day. At last, a light dawned on the Indian. He glanced up with a gleam in his eye and answered, "Oh, I see. Your God comes one day a week; My God is with me every day and all the time."*

Robert Coles, who was an eminent physician at Harvard Medical School, was deeply interested in the spiritual life of children and spent a year on the Hopi reservation researching this topic. At first, he visited the tribal school and spoke with the Native American boys and girls, but without success. The children were reticent, reluctant to share. One day, one of the Hopi women at the school told Coles that he was wasting his time. The children would never speak openly with him at school because when they come to school, she said, they leave who they really are at the door. She then went on to say that if you want them to speak with you openly, you must go to their homes. This he did.

---

*   Seton, *The Gospel of the Redman*, p. 5.

In a subsequent conversation at the home of a ten-year-old Hopi girl, Robert Coles asked her about her beliefs.

"The sky watches us and listens to us. It talks to us and hopes we are ready to talk back."

She went on to say, "The teacher told us that the sky is where the God of the Anglos lives. She asked us where our God lives?"

I said, "I don't know." I was telling the truth. "Our God is the Sun and the Moon, too. Our God is our people, too, if we remember to stay connected to the land."

"Did you explain this to your teacher?" Coles asked.

"No."

"Why?" asked Coles.

"Because she thinks God is a person. If I told her, she'd give us that smile."

"What smile?" Cole asked.

"The smile that says to us, 'You are cute, but you are dumb. You are different and you're all wrong.'"

Coles suggested, "Perhaps you could have explained that to her the way you explained it to me."

"We tried that a long time ago; our people spoke to the Anglos.... [So] we smile and say 'yes' to them all the time and we pray for them."*

Our children today need the awareness that the Great Spirit is everywhere, in the rising moon and in the sun overhead, in the clouds, and particularly in Mother Earth with her four legged and winged creatures and the trees and stones. This would provide an antidote for much of what ails children today. Working with the earth is healing, as is time outdoors. Being in the quiet solitude of nature helps to offset the busy-ness of children's schedules. But more than this, the beauty and wonder of nature should not pass us

---

*   Coles, *The Spiritual Life of Children*, p. 25.

by. We need to reconnect with a natural world that is filled with meaning.

The intricate interconnectedness of all life has always been part of the Native American's understanding. These understandings have been beautifully explained by the botanist Robin Wall Kimmerer in her extraordinary book, *Braiding Sweetgrass,* and in her Ted Talk, "Reclaiming the Honorable Harvest." Her experiments and research at the State University in New York substantiate the Indigenous understanding of the interconnectedness of all life: how buffalo saliva contains a chemical that causes prairie grass to regenerate more quickly; how the complementary colors of purple asters and goldenrod flowers serve as pollinator magnets, perfectly suited to the unique eye structure of bees.* This interconnectedness is such an important spiritual idea because it helps to redefine our sense of self, and our humanity. There is much in these Native understandings that we urgently need today, particularly gratitude for all that is around us. Robin Wall Kimmerer's research shows that the presence of thankful, caring human beings in the natural world actually furthers the wellbeing of the plant kingdom.**

A former colleague said that "gratitude is a barometer of soul health." If this is so, children today are not as healthy as they should be. Parents and teachers know this through first-hand experience, as so much today is taken for granted in our time of an extreme sense of entitlement. We need to find a health-giving remedy for our children. But that remedy must start with us, the adults, and not with a lecture, and certainly not with a sermon. We must

---

*   Kimmerer, *Braiding Sweetgrass,* pp. 45, 46.
**   Ibid pp. 159–163.

begin to work on our own awareness and reconnect with our own spiritual and religious life so that it quietly finds its expression in our family where it can make a lasting impression on our children.

Our times are calling for a greater awareness of the spirit, but it must be new and alive. How should we celebrate the year with its turning points, its holidays? How should we honor birth and death in our families and in our friend's families? What spiritual and religious understandings should we cultivate in our children and how do we do this sensitively, but effectively? In short, how do we live our own lives so that we set an ongoing example for our children? These are important questions facing parents today.

Our young children are inclined to believe. We have a responsibility to safeguard their sense of the heavenly. In the early grade-school years, there is an openness to the mystery of life. They encounter this mystery repeatedly in the curriculum, in the creation myths and stories of all the ancient civilizations, and they quietly internalize these stories. We need to nurture that awareness, and certainly not minimize it through our explanations.

This can be complicated. Many parents today, when asked about their religious orientation, say they are not religious. Others will simply say they are atheists because there is no belief system with which they align. Certainly, a good portion of our adult society leans in this direction. Perhaps if we are open and attentive, more inclined to wonder, we will begin to resonate with this statement by the environmental author, Janisse Ray.

I no longer say I am an atheist. The universe is too marvelous and magical, and I have seen too much of providence and the inexplicable not to believe in spirit. Something more than a heartbeat left my grandmother's body when she died. The idea that spirit exists, that some things are not what they appear pleases me. Some things lie beyond that realm of human knowledge.*

An awareness like this can help us to guide our children in the right direction. Above all our children need to feel at home in the world. This sense of being at home is an inner experience, about much more than geography. It is about belonging and being seen. Unfortunately, what many young people experience today is a growing sense of alienation and loneliness that leaves them with the feeling that they don't belong. The words that are often attached to this sense of alienation are terms like "lost," "adrift," "at sea," terms that show how far they feel from a spiritual home.

Our young people see so much pain and suffering in the world: the wars, the terrorist attacks, the shootings, the disasters, the poverty, the heartache. They see it all and it affects them. We have to help them see that the opposite is also true, that the world is still a place of remarkable beauty with millions upon millions of good people.

The alienation of young people is, at its heart, a spiritual question, one of lost connection. For so many today, the world they meet lacks meaning. Our conventional schools, which have such a formative influence, offer little in this regard. The common curriculum in most mainstream schools is composed of an array of unrelated subjects without coherence. The best that it can offer students is an assortment of skills and curious facts about nature and

---

* Ray, *Wild Card Quilt*, p. 76.

historical events that leaves them with little lasting appreciation and wonder for the world they inhabit.

Sadly, it is not easy for parents to counteract this loss of meaning when our pervading culture is fragmented and misleading. We need to find a way to clarify our own spiritual awareness, and to let it live in our homes, in the surround, so that our children sense it. These spiritual beliefs need to become the unshakable foundation upon which we stand. Without a sense that the challenges we face are significant opportunities for growth and not random events, our children will be undermined by anxiety. Like these lines of Rilke's, we must help our children see that no matter what happens, we are held. This is the bedrock of resilience.

> So you mustn't be frightened, if a sadness rises in front of you, larger than any you have seen.... You must realize that something is happening to you, that life has not forgotten you, that it holds you in the palm of its hand and will not let you fall.*

---

*   Rilke, *Letters to a Young Poet*, p. 8.

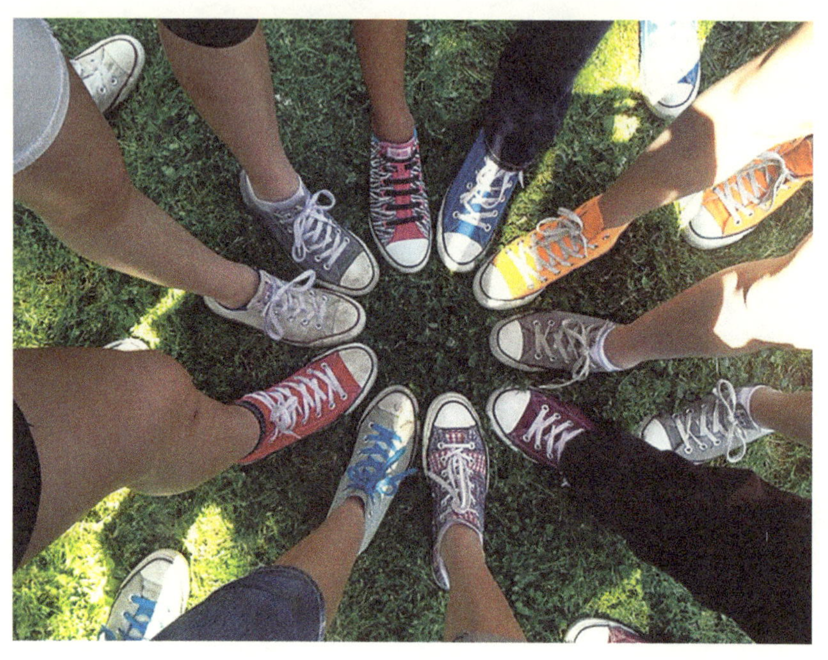

PART THREE

MIDDLE SCHOOL AND MORE

17

The Twelve-Year Change

It was sixth grade, and I was taking my students to the Shenandoah National Park in Virginia to explore caves and to hike up some of the oldest mountains in the country. As we headed west out of Washington, D.C., we began to see the mountains in the distance—a pale blue ridge on the horizon. I pointed this out to the students and waited for their response when I suddenly heard a voice, "Look there's a Mercedes S-Class Coupe and there's a BMW Z4." Disappointment filled my teacher's soul as I realized that my students had little or no interest in the mountains, at least not compared to their interest in automobiles. All I could think was that here I was, bringing them all this way, and all they were interested in were cars. But I stopped myself, suddenly aware that in sixth grade we study Rome and that my sixth-grade students were Romans—prosaic, worldly, and definitely materialistic.

Any teacher who works with the students from first grade to eighth cannot miss the significant developmental change that occurs in middle school. Something starts to shift in sixth grade and feels so different in seventh, and eighth. What is this change all about and how should teachers understand it and address it?

In his small but important book *The Education of the Child*, Rudolf Steiner states that children are not born just once, but rather that they experience multiple births when entirely new aspects of who they are emerge. Aside from the physical birth, there is the birth that occurs around the age of six or seven. This change corresponds to the change of teeth and the start of grade school. Seven or so years later, around thirteen or fourteen, another birth occurs. This next birth is accompanied by all of the emotional intensity and unpredictability of adolescence, as well as the beginning of clear, objective, and fairly critical thinking. Waldorf teachers anticipate the dramatic change that accompanies a student's growing maturity and this is reflected in the teaching approach in the high school with the new emphasis that is placed on critical thinking and independent judgment.

But in one of his seminal lecture series, *Practical Advice to Teachers*, Steiner indicated that these changes begin earlier than high school.

> During the twelfth and thirteenth year, the spirit and soul elements in the human being are strengthened. What, in spiritual science, we are accustomed to calling the astral body permeates the etheric (or life body) and unites with it…manifesting in a peculiar manner through the etheric by permeating it and invigorating it between the twelfth and thirteenth year.*

Another way to think about this is to imagine a river like the Mississippi beginning in the north with cool, clear water. This clear water represents all the life and vitality of the early elementary school time. As that river makes the long journey toward the Gulf of Mexico and high school, something changes. Somewhere around the sixth grade, the water starts to turn brackish as a new element enters. Salt

---

* Steiner, *Practical Advice to Teachers,* p. 107.

water from the Gulf makes its way upstream and permeates the fresh water coming from the north. Sixth grade is slightly brackish, but seventh grade is decidedly so, and by eighth grade, the students are very brackish, and like the river itself, they are ready to spread out and flow into the larger waters of high school.

The middle school is a mixture of these two streams and any teacher who works with this age experiences this blending and the needs this blending generates. To teach well in the middle school, we still need to meet a good many of the needs that the students had when they were younger, and at the same time we must also meet the emerging needs of an older student.

The early grade-school student's needs are well documented. Perhaps the most notable is the need for a clear, consistent schedule in which the predictability of class patterns and events provides grounding and reassurance, and at the same time fosters a growing awareness of school routines and practices. We usually call this quality "rhythm." In addition, there is the need for consistent structure so that young students come to know what is expected of them and can rest assured in that knowledge. Waldorf teachers call this aspect "form," akin to format and formality. But what must also be kept in mind is that middle-school students chafe at each of these qualities as they grow older. The consistent routine seems dull in its predictability, and structure and formality seem restrictive. Yet, middle-school students still need both, just in a different way.

Another important piece for the younger student is the class teacher/student relationship. In the early grades the class teacher is a significant part of the bedrock upon which everything seems to rest—there at the start and close of each day as well as lunch time and recess to care for the students. When all goes well, young students revere their teachers in a most pronounced way and accept their warm and loving authority. But the needs of the adolescent are harder to delineate.

A good way to consider these new, emerging needs is to explore our best memories of adolescence. I am convinced that as students we knew when our needs were being met. Whenever I have asked parents and teachers for their best memories of junior high and high school, some striking recollections have been shared. These recollections are always connected with memorable teachers. What I have heard repeatedly is that these memorable teachers knew their subject and were passionate about their teaching. In addition, they often held their students to a high standard, and what becomes clear is that the adolescent wants to learn and wants to be challenged.

Other memories describe the unique way a teacher dressed, their mannerisms and their teaching style—teachers who threw caution to the wind and taught original lessons, teachers who wanted to know their students on a deeper level and afforded them considerable respect. In turn, the adolescent students want to know who their teacher is as an individual and what their life is like outside of school. As much as the young students want to look up to their teachers, adolescents want to relate in a more horizontal manner. Continually, adolescent students will seek out the teachers or coaches they admire and stop by their classroom or their office during free time or at the end of the day, hoping to build this connection.

Because middle school is a blending of both streams—the fresh water of the early grades and the salt water of the teenage years—it is necessary for the instructional programs to blend the needs of both ages. Middle-school programs should offer academic challenges to the students, but this should be done in a way that deepens learning rather than just accelerating the acquisition of knowledge. Skills classes become increasingly important in middle school so that students have another teacher with whom to develop mastery of a subject. The specialty teacher is called on to challenge, surprise, and relate to these students in a different manner and still meet the need for rhythm, repetition, and routine. A middle-school English teacher at our school did a fine job of blending the two needs. He held the students to a high standard with unwavering demands. Yet, each week he would do this in the same way. Vocabulary homework was due every Tuesday, accompanied by a test, and the reading assignment for literature was due on Thursday. This consistent routine provided clarity and predictability for the middle-school students who often have a great deal of difficulty remembering when assignments need to be handed in.

Academic subjects like mathematics and English are surely not the only subjects in which middle-school students need to be held to a higher standard. Art is another area where more should be expected of the students. The Renaissance art reproductions, done in grade seven, are a wonderful challenge. Similarly, the main lesson book illustrations, the portraits in a history study, the illustrations of demonstrations in a science block, the lettering and coloring for maps in a geography block, should all be of the highest quality.

The truth is that it takes constant vigilance to expect middle-school students to produce quality work. Many students work on the premise that, if they resist giving their best long enough, the adults will give in. That's why it is so important for middle-school students to have a team of teachers. It takes a team effort to help students be responsible right through the end of eighth grade.

Another well-respected English teacher at our school would regularly show up at the door of my middle school classroom at lunchtime. She would stand in the doorway and read the names of three or four students who either "forgot" to do their homework or had not completed their assignment carefully. She was "inviting" them to spend their lunchtime with her in the library. I cheered inwardly. Her dedication helped the students know that, when she gave an assignment, she took it seriously and was willing to do the extra work of rounding them up, even sacrificing her lunch hour so they could make amends. I valued her help and the students respected her dedication, and, needless to say, their work habits improved. It is important to note that my students admired and greatly enjoyed their classes with both of these English teachers.

There are particular qualities that make for successful middle-school teaching. (Humor, of course, is huge.) One of the unspoken qualities commonly shared by good middle-school teachers is that they like the students and remember what it was like to be a teenager. That can make a world of difference.

Seventh grade can be a difficult time for teachers who have taken their class from grade one. A colleague would refer to seventh grade as "the tunnel." You know that there is light at the end of seventh grade, you just can't see it dur-ing the year. When I was a new class teacher I struggled with this age. I could see only the deterioration of habits that I had worked so hard to instill and the constant preoccupa-tion with modern cultural life, which seemed to increase in importance with each passing day.

In the spring of seventh grade my first class put on a play, "The Devil and Daniel Webster," based on a short story by Stephen Vincent Benet. In this story, a young farmer, Jabez Stone, sells his soul to the devil in exchange for prosperity. After the sale of his soul, his farm prospers, he is elected to the state senate, and he becomes engaged to a young woman he has long fancied. On the day of his wedding, the contract that he signed has run its seven-year course and the devil shows up to collect his due. In extreme distress, Jabez Stone goes to his friend and wedding guest, Daniel Webster, and explains his situation. Mr. Webster, a distinguished lawyer and orator, decides to take the case and represent Stone and begins by disputing the contract, saying that his client is not obligated to honor this agreement because the Constitution states that an American citizen need not pay homage to a foreign lord. The devil counters by saying that he is not a foreigner and that when the first slave ship landed, he was on board. When the first wrong was done to the Natives, he was there as well. "Frankly, Mr. Webster," he states, "my name is older in this country than yours." Outmaneuvered, Webster demands a trial for his client—"any judge, any jury." The devil complies and conjures up the most despica-ble jury from America's past: Blackbeard, Benedict Arnold, Simon Girty, and more. He even calls forth the judge from the Salem Witch Trials. The seventh-grade students love playing the zombie-like jury and need no coaching on how to answer in unison in a deep monotone, similar to how they liked to recite most poetry and the morning verse. As Webster begins to plead his case, he is put off and then repelled by the unseemly nature of this jury. And yet, the more antipathy he feels for the jury, the more antipathy they mirror back. Finally, Webster realizes that he must appeal to their best selves, he must help them remember who they really are and what it means to be human. As he does this, the jurors begin to soften and are won over.*

It was during this play that I suddenly realized that it is the same with the seventh graders. The teachers who like them, who help them remember their best selves, who can appreciate (within reason) some of the foolish things they do, are the very teachers the students like, and their behavior becomes less problematic. The teachers who notice only the difficulties are given many more opportunities to experience those behaviors.

All challenging situations offer us an opportunity for growth. For me, teaching in the middle school provided those opportunities in a big way. Oddly enough, this occurred one time when I was teaching a class other than my own. Although my primary assignment was to teach third grade at the time, as part of my faculty responsibilities I was assigned to teach math and calligraphy to the sixth grade. This sixth grade was a class that I found particularly challenging and, to make matters worse, two of the three periods for my work with them were in the afternoon. I wondered what I had done to the scheduling person in a past life to merit this assignment.

---

* Benet, http://gutenberg.net.au/ebooks06/0602901h.html.

This class proved to be so difficult that the normal protocol, such as a teacher standing in the front of the room greeting the class with "Good afternoon, Sixth Grade," to which they would reply, "Good afternoon, Mr. Petrash," was not easy. Instead, I found the students away from their desks or walking around the room. They hardly noticed that I was trying to begin our class. I was at a loss. I could begin my class by disciplining students. I could even ask the main culprit(s) to leave the room, but that would have destroyed the small semblance of goodwill that prevailed and would have left the class disliking me and, more important, me disliking myself. Something different was called for, but I had no idea what it was. I was desperate and fortunately for me, desperation has often been my impetus for innovation.

At the start of the next class, I did not begin with a formal greeting. Rather, when I entered the room, I walked directly to the blackboard and started drawing. "Take out your books," I announced, "and start drawing Math Woman." There she was on the board, "Math Woman," dressed like a super hero with a cape, leotard, tights, tunic, and matching eurythmy shoes.

Now the students were intrigued, and with some encouragement they opened their books, took out their colored pencils, and started drawing. Then I wrote on the board, "Math Woman says, 'When you add fractions, you must have common denominators.'" This was followed by some demonstration examples and a worksheet. We had begun our extensive fraction review (important work in grade six), and in each class Math Woman would appear at the start of the lesson and introduce new review material. Her hairstyle would change, and her super hero outfit came in different colors, but she was a mainstay in our class. The students began each class by drawing and writing, but within ten minutes they were ready to learn and our classes improved markedly.

One of the students, whom I will just call "N," was particularly snarky. He sat in the back of the room and made comments from time to time about the other students. His most derogatory remark, which he reserved for the cooperative students, was "Waldorfian," as in "You are so Waldorfian."

One afternoon, while the students were drawing Math Woman at the start of class, I happened to walk by N's desk. His colored pencil case was open and it was a revelation. All of his colored pencils were sharpened and looked brand new. What's more, they were all lined up in rainbow order. I was surprised by the care he took with his pencils because he seemed not to care about anything, and I exclaimed, "N, Look at your pencils. They're in rainbow order. You're Waldorfian." He immediately slammed his case shut and replied vehemently, "I am not." But he had been seen. "You're Waldorfian," I repeated and the class chuckled. And from that day on, my relationship with this student and with the class was filled with much more warmth. They had been a challenging class, for sure, but they had made me a better teacher. The truth is they became a favorite specialty class to teach. In sixth grade we are still called on to be "authorities," but it is often the original work that we "author" and create for the benefit of our students that makes all the difference.

Just as a footnote, I saw this student recently. He's almost forty years old. He smiled at me and said, "You know' I still take care of my pencils."

What became eminently clear to me was that the twelfth year/sixth grade was the beginning of a transition and that now my teaching needed to change. I also came to see that I should involve my students more fully in the lessons. Finding the right question to stimulate a rich classroom discussion became as important as the material I was going to present. And I must say that I have been awed by the depth of the discussions that have taken place in my classroom and how thirteen and fourteen-year-old students can just rise to the occasion when you invite them to speak about what they think. Sound thinking does not happen overnight. It too, develops gradually over time.

Our children will need to develop dynamic thinking— thinking they can depend on—if they are going to meet the challenges they will inevitably face in life. They will need to be keenly attentive and to know what they think. As early as seventh grade the students are beginning to have thought- ful opinions (and yes, sometimes not so thoughtful). Most of all I needed to remind myself that my students were giv- ing birth to a new stage of development, and although this stage matures mostly in high school and college, it is making its presence felt in seventh and eighth grade. As I became a more experienced teacher, I learned to be on the lookout for signs that this change was beginning and to meet this change always with a smile and with the understanding that this development was just right.

I remember the time in eighth grade when I was speaking with my class about our eighth-grade trip. They had probably brought the subject up to delay the start of main lesson, and I was telling them a little about what I was considering, which was not going on an extravagant trip to England or Hawaii, or a cruise to Cancún (their suggestion). Just then, one of the students raised her hand and asked, "Why do **you** choose where we go on our trip?" I didn't take offense. I only thought that is a legitimate question from a student who had turned fourteen more than six months before. The next day I came to school and presented my class with a choice. We could travel north from D.C., visit New York City, and then make our way to Boston and Concord and visit colonial history sites. Or we could head south to Williamsburg and Jamestown and end up on the Outer Banks of North Carolina, where it would be warmer, and we could visit historical sites and spend some time on the beach. Needless to say, they unanimously chose to go south, which was my choice as well. The important part was giving them some choice. This is what the adolescent entering this next phase of development desires. That's why they appreciate electives even when they choose an activity because their friends have chosen it.

Another time when this new awareness in one of my students made itself felt was when I was giving a homework assignment at the end of a main lesson in grade eight. I was describing how I wanted the students to do the assignment (probably a map), how I wanted it labeled and colored, what kind of border, etc., when one of my most dependable and cooperative students asked, "Do I still have to do the assignment the way you ask, or can I do it the way I think is best?" This was a great question coming from a student with a new awareness rising out of this new phase of development. My take-away was always to be waiting and watching and welcoming this change, and not resenting that it seemed to question my authority as a teacher.

This new understanding also helped with the discipline in my class in the older grades, which also had to come from a place of objectivity, exactly what the students want at this age. But one of the ways this happened in my class-room was quite unexpected. I had asked a good friend, Donald Bufano, an experienced middle-school and high-school teacher, what he did when his students asked the same questions incessantly: "Can we have extra recess?" "Can we change seats?" "Do we have to have homework tonight?" These seemingly benign questions can become tiresome and contentious. Donald's reply was surprising. "I use the Magic Eight Ball." This is an enlarged black plastic pool ball that answers questions. You shake the ball vigorously and then you turn it over where there is a small plastic window in which answers appear such as: "No Way!" "You Bet!" "Not Today!" So I purchased a Magic Eight Ball, and it never let us down. Like rock, paper, scissors, it moved decision making to a higher plane. Of course, I didn't use the Magic Eight Ball for bigger questions, like: "Is our main lesson book really due on Monday?" "Do we have to do a geography report on a country in Asia?" But from time to time with the small, "picky" questions it worked so well.

One of my students would invariably approach me at lunchtime and ask for some of my salad. She always had her own lunch, but found mine more appetizing. I would just reply, "Please get the Magic Eight Ball." I would shake it, turn it over, and invariably it would say, "Not Today" or "Forget About It." Finally, my salad-loving student said with exasperation, "The Magic Eight Ball doesn't like me." Her classmates and I just had to smile because it was funny how her luck ran and how she accepted this. I was always grateful for moments that kept the mood in the class buoyant in middle school.

18

TAKING HARD TO HEART

Most of us are destined to failure,
which is a form of suffering.
How to turn the lead of our defeat
into the gold of something else,
is the object of religious alchemy.
Not the only one,
but the one most of us are interested in.
— SYDNEY CARTER*

At the end of a long day of parent/teacher conferences, a colleague told my wife, "I saw Jack this afternoon, and I have never seen anyone look like that and still be standing." Clearly, Waldorf education can ask a great deal of its teachers. We feel this at the end of a school day, depleted with a weariness similar to what parents feel when they finally get their children to bed. There is fatigue on many levels. It's physical—our feet and back can ache and our shoulders are tight. Some days at three o'clock we look pale and worn, more than a little disheveled, like someone who's been left out in the wind all day. In addition, we've given on a soul level. Every time we have turned to patience and checked our immediate response for a better one, we have used our best forces. We have also done this every time we've set aside our own needs and attended to the needs of the children. And we have given of ourselves spiritually. How many teachers

---

* Carter, *Dance in the Dark*, p. 143.

know those dark hours of the night when we lie awake in bed worried about one of our students long after the school day has ended.

The silver lining in this is that we feel this way because we have offered our best forces and our best teaching efforts on behalf of our students. We are in need of being replenished, and that's on the good days. But what about the more discouraging days when uninspired teaching meets students who feel no compelling desire to attend to our lessons? Where do we turn on those days?

I have always believed on the "bad days" that I must look first at my own role in what has gone wrong in my classroom. What did I miss? Which children did I misread? What was flawed in my lesson plan? Was it too factual? Did it lack the necessary imagination? These are just some of the questions I have asked myself at the end of a discouraging day, and it was always better if I was able to pose these questions in the quiet of my classroom a little after three o'clock.

I have always loved my classroom—with my students especially, but also without them. Those quiet times at the end of the school day when I could sit at my desk and decompress were important to my teaching. During those times, I could open my notebook, look at my lesson plan, and note where things went awry. Sometimes it was early in a lesson when some students rolled their eyes at a poem or a song that they thought was "babyish." Other times it was because my well-intentioned attempt to review yesterday's work went on too long, engaging some but not all of the students. There was all manner of reasons for my flawed lessons, but having time to reflect enabled me to isolate the problem and to adjust my next day's teaching. Without time for reflection these adjustments might not have occurred.

On occasion, I have thought that my teaching situation could be compared to a saturated solution in chemistry. Each school day would absorb the work with the children. To that more solute was added (recess duty, an assembly program, a visitor…) and with a little stirring that, too, would get dissolved into the mix. When the unexpected occurred—a disagreement between two children, a fire drill, or an unplanned substitution—simple stirring was not enough to absorb all that was being added. But turn the heat up under the solution and continue stirring, and these events would be dissolved as well. Sometimes, by three o'clock I had been heated up and stirred up repeatedly. Those were the days when I could feel my head spinning just like the solution, on the verge of being super-saturated. However, when I could pause at the end of one of those days and sit quietly at my desk or simply work in the classroom washing the blackboard, sweeping the floor, or straightening the rows, my thoughts could begin to precipitate out of the solution and slowly settle as new understandings.

It is also possible with a saturated solution to set within it a "seed crystal," like a bit of sugar crystal that you hang from a string and that allows a larger crystal, a new understanding, to form. For me, the seed crystal that I needed to place into the mix has always been one of the essential principles of Waldorf education.

When I trained to be a Waldorf teacher, I was only twenty-three years old. I brought enthusiasm to my studies, but probably not as much consciousness. It was only after I started teaching a first grade that I realized the questions

I should have asked in my training, questions about form drawing, watercolor painting, nature stories, and more. However, what I did take away with my graduate degree in Waldorf education was an understanding of the threefold nature of the human being and how every lesson should balance in an age-appropriate way thinking, feeling, and willing. This became my touchstone in evaluating my "failed lessons." Was there enough purposeful activity? Did I teach sufficiently to the feeling life of my students through art, music, imagination, and story? Did I find a way in every single lesson to bring my students something new to engage their thinking? Over time this understanding crystallized into the ability to read my students.*

The threefold nature of the child was not the only educational principle that guided me in my reflection; it was just the first. I also considered the importance of "breathing" in my lessons with the understanding that wide-awake, quiet attention in the classroom (breathing in) needed to be balanced with active, hands-on dynamic participation (breathing out).

Several years ago, I heard an education professor from Wittenburg University, Lowell Monke, state that traditional American schools were based on a factory model. Our school buildings looked like factories and the method of instruction often resembled assembly-line production. The children arrive at 8:30 and we expect to turn on the "learning switch," and they should learn until 3:00, when they are permitted to turn the switch off. Needless to say, children don't learn like this. Their learning is more closely aligned with nature, and in nature there is a continual ebb and flow, more like a sine

---

* See https://www.youtube.com/watch?v=imaW-TabxOE&t=62s.

curve. I had to ask myself if my ineffective lesson lacked the proper vacillation. Had I provided my students with the necessary moments "not to pay attention" to what I was saying and simply immerse themselves in drawing or writing? Or had I made the fatal mistake of talking too much, forgetting that moments of hands-on activity enable the students to pay even better attention later on.

Looking at my lessons in this reflective way, *taking hard to heart*, was the turning point for me because it led me more fully into my inner work as a teacher by focusing on what I needed for my own inner development to become a better teacher. Surely my students deserved that. When I took to heart my tendency to talk longer than I should and worked on controlling my speech, a breakthrough occurred. I discovered that Rudolf Steiner's daily exercise for Monday was to control speech. This was part of Steiner's application of the Buddha's Eightfold Path. Each day of the week had a particular exercise, and I was delighted to find that the other daily exercises could help me be a better teacher, as well.

On Tuesday, the exercise is Right Action, and we are urged to adjust ourselves to the needs of others. On this day, more than any other, I would allow my students' questions and expressed interests to direct the lesson. If a meaningful question was asked, I was willing to set aside my lesson plan and take up the question. We would close our books and begin considering the new question right then and there. Needless to say, real learning took place.

Wednesday's exercise, Right Standpoint, is about keeping all things in balance, a good guiding principle. On Thursdays, we are asked to exercise Right Judgment and do all things to the best of our ability. Thursday was the day, more than any other, when I held my students to the highest standard. If the recitation of a poem or the morning verse was half-hearted it would not pass on a Thursday. I would simply say (pleasantly enough), "I know you can do better. Let's try that again." The same was often said on that day to individual students about their compositions, their math assignments, their homework, and their illustrations.

Friday was Right Remembrance, but I just thought of it as "memory day," the day when teachers all over the country in all manner of schools, are asking students to recall what they learned during the week for the test they were about to take. But truthfully, my favorite part of Friday was something my class and I called "Golden Oldies." In the opening of our Friday lesson my students could request poems, verses, or songs that we had done in the early grades, and we would recite those lines and recall those days with a smile.

However, the most important part of Steiner's adaptation of Buddha's Eightfold Path was the exercise that could be done each day. This is called Right Meditation:

> Each day, at the same time if possible
> Turn inward and take stock of life,
> Test one's way of life,
> Run over one's store of knowledge,
> Ponder one's duties and responsibilities,
> Consider the aim and true purposes of life,
> Reflect on one's own imperfections and mistakes.
> In short, distinguish what is significant,
> Distinguish what is of lasting value,
> And renew one's resolve to take up worthwhile tasks.*

---

* Steiner, *The Illustrated Buddha Path*, Friday / Right Meditation.

Having a daily practice is so important for a Waldorf teacher. We need time each day to reconnect with our best selves. Prior to digital innovation, analog radio tuners had a little arrow to indicate when reception of a station's broadcast was received most clearly. My inner life is similar in the sense that there are repeatedly times when my "reception," my connection with the spiritual world wavers. Each day I need to realign myself through reading, reflection, meditation or contemplative prayer. I need to recall my challenges as a teacher and to remember what I don't want to do in my classroom. It is inevitable that we will make mistakes. We are not expected to be perfect, but our mistakes should not fall into a habitual pattern. Our students are sure to notice this when it happens.

The details of a daily practice should be entirely up to the individual teacher. It doesn't matter what time of the day we choose as long as it works, and it doesn't matter what we choose to read, only that it inspires and uplifts us and connects us to our best self. It is our intention to do this each day for the good of our children and for the betterment of our teaching that matters. Our daily practice needs to become a habit.

Waldorf teaching is a calling, not a job. You can tell that when you hear the stories of how teachers come to this work, "how they just knew" like love at first sight, how unexpected, serendipitous events brought them to the school, how their children brought them, or how a friend introduced them to the school. These encounters are moments of destiny. Our hearts are won over, and anytime we give our hearts to an undertaking, it changes us, and that transformational aspect is at the heart of our humanity.

Being a Waldorf teacher will change us. This is true with all of the important commitments in our lives. Marriage and raising children are the same. In the end we will be different people than the ones we were when we started out. The important question is what kind of change are we seeking and how do we support that change?

In his book, *Education of the Child*, Rudolf Steiner speaks about two types of change.* The first he compares to the movement of the minute hand on a clock. This change happens quickly and involves a change in ideas. It is the kind of change that occurs when young people attend college. They return home with new judgments, new vocabulary, and new values. But that change does not always occur on a deeper level.

There is a second type of change and this resembles the movement of the hour hand. This is a change in character, temperament, memory, and habits. These changes are harder to achieve, but worth so much more. There are two ways to achieve this change. It can come about through a crisis that we experience in our lives when illness or heartache lays us low and we emerge a different person. In the book *Geeks and Geezers*, the authors note that this is a characteristic of remarkable business leaders. They have often had crucible experiences (like Steve Jobs when he was fired from Apple), moments when their life was melted down, when unnecessary dross was removed and they emerged chastened and renewed.** When we meet people who have gone through this kind of experience and are transformed, we are heartened.

---

* Steiner, *The Education of the Child*, p. 13.
** Bennis and Thomas, *Geeks and Geezers*, pp. 17–19.

It is also possible for us to take up spiritual practices that can be done to assist our inner development. Perhaps, in Waldorf circles the six supplementary exercises are the best known. These practices work to enhance our inner lives through monthly exercises. The first involves the training of our thinking.

A number of years ago in a seventh-grade physiology lesson, I asked my students if the tongue was a voluntary muscle. I explained to them that whenever I chip a tooth or lose a filling, my tongue continually returns to the sharp edge of the tooth even though I don't want it to. Then I asked them how many times they end up saying things they don't mean to say. We had a good discussion about the tongue and then one of the boys asked, "What about my mind? Is that a voluntary muscle? Because thoughts run through my mind continually, even though I don't want them to." It was at that moment that I did something unexpected, something I had never done with a class. I went to my supply closet and took out two boxes of brand-new lead pencils, which I distributed to my students. Then I explained to my students that I wanted them to focus their thinking on this pencil for the next few minutes and have their thoughts continuously pertain to the pencil—its length and thickness, its six-sided shape, its school-bus yellow color, the small pink rubber cylinder at one end, the carved cone with an exposed graphite tip that would be at the other end when it is sharpened—how pencils are used, why they are used, how long they last, and more. After this exercise, in which they controlled their thinking, my students were much more focused in main lesson than usual.

Today's students—whose lives abound with continual texting, music, YouTube and TikTok videos, Instagram postings, and more—are clearly in need of more focused thinking. But so are we as adults. Sound, focused thinking is the starting point for a healthy inner life. This is the objective of the first month of these six exercises.

The second exercise is for the development of the will and asks that we perform a certain task at the same time every day during the second month. Our ability to consciously repeat an activity is at the heart of successful Waldorf teaching, for no other educational program, except maybe Teach for America, will ask for as much effort from a teacher. Our ability to prepare our lessons regularly for two hours each day will test our determination and our will.

The power and potential that is contained in our will is well represented by the story in *The Man Who Planted Trees*.* It recounts the life of a simple shepherd in France after World War I. His village and the land around his village had been devastated by the war, leaving the people dispirited. Each day the shepherd would take his flock into the countryside to graze, and while he walked with the sheep he would fill his pockets with acorns. When he approached the treeless area where the battles had occurred, he would use his shepherd's staff to make holes to plant the acorns he had gathered. He did this each and every day and after a number of years the trees began to return in abundance. This kind of change to the Earth, which occurs even more slowly than the movement of an hour hand, shows how human beings, through their determined activity, can indeed change the world.

---

*   Giono, *The Man Who Planted Trees*.

The third, fourth, and fifth months' exercises focus on inner soul qualities such as equanimity, positivity, and openness. They are perfectly described in Michael Lipson's insightful book, *The Stairway of Surprise*. Lipson clearly, concisely, and engagingly describes all six of the exercises as a way of developing what he calls our "human extra," our ability to make more of ourselves through our conscious, intentional effort. One of my favorite parts of the book pertains to the fifth month's exercise—openness. There, Lipson describes a morning ride with his young son:

> We were starting to drive to a friend's house, and my son Rody, then five, announced, "We're going to school!"
>
> "No," I said, "The beginning of our trip today is toward school, but we're going farther, to Steve's house. We're not going to school."
>
> "Oh, yes, we are!" insisted Rody. "This is the way to school. We're going to school."
>
> It went back and forth like this a few times. Finally, I just said. "Let's see."
>
> The moment came when we didn't take the last turn to school, but drove on past.
>
> Rody looked around in delighted astonishment.
>
> "I was wrong!" he shouted, utterly gleeful.*

Lipson goes on to say, "This is a talent we lose in adulthood: the ability to find genuine pleasure in being wrong." I certainly didn't respond in this way often enough in faculty meetings or with my class.

Students hope that their teachers will be willing to change. We are on a path of development and are called on to be better people in the end than we were when we started. It is essential that we have a daily practice to support this

---

* Lipson, *Stairway of Surprise*, p. 90.

development and to help us remember that our students always know when we are doing the important work of taking hard to heart.

19

Goldilocks Had it Right All Along

Over the years, my understanding of how to teach has been honed repeatedly. What now remains are a few essential understandings that have sustained my work. Sometimes these understandings express themselves in surprising ways. Of late, I have been left with the impression that Goldilocks had it right all along.

As Waldorf teachers we have to work continually with opposites, such as breathing in and breathing out; stillness and movement; form and freedom. The list goes on. Our primary assignment as teachers is to stand between these polarities and find the right balance. The assessment can change from day to day, month to month, and certainly from year to year. We are continually asked to be conscious of the interplay of these polarities as we teach.

Safe, but Not Too Safe

Educators know that students in all schools learn most effectively when they feel that their classroom is safe and predictable. Establishing this secure and dependable environment is particularly the work of the preschool and early grade school teachers. Creating a protective, homelike atmosphere with a familiar routine enables the children to relax and to be fully receptive to their school experience. The gentle repetition and sequence of activities and the quiet anticipation of experiences like circle, story time, and snack help the younger children acclimate to the school day. During the course of the early grades, the students depend on the rhythm of the school day. However, what I realized in the upper grades was that the opposite understanding was also necessary. When the students are older, a certain tension brought on by change—in short, a lack of safety—needed to be added to my teaching repertoire.

Let me offer an example. I never attended a Waldorf school. I was educated in the New York City public schools, and I went to a fairly good high school in Manhattan. By all accounts, Stuyvesant High School offered its students a sound education. One of my first experiences there left a lasting impression. It occurred in my chemistry class. My teacher, who was simply referred to as "The Colonel," was an elderly gentleman with a deep southern accent, definitely uncommon in New York.

In our first class, the Colonel handed out a paper with a list of a dozen or so basic elements in the Periodic Table and told us to learn their valences. I was not yet a conscientious student, and so that evening I did not even look at the list. When I came into class the next morning, the Colonel handed each student a blank piece of paper and told us to put our name at the top and to number from one to ten. He then proceeded to give us the names of ten elements—hydrogen, oxygen, sodium, potassium, carbon, etc.—which we were to write down with the corresponding valences. When we were finished, he collected the quizzes and stood at his desk and marked them right then and there. Then he read a series of names: Epstein, Medina, Peller, Petrash.... There were four or five of us. Then he said, "If your name was called, stand up and leave the classroom. There is an empty room next door. Do not come back until you've learned your valences." Needless to say, I learned my valences and did every subsequent assignment that the Colonel gave in a timelier manner.

I believe that teachers often teach to the kind of student they had been in school. I know I did. I recall teaching eighth grade and handing out the novel *Johnny Tremaine* to my students. I assigned the first two chapters for homework, yet I knew that there were students in my class who were not going to open the book that evening.

The next morning, like the Colonel, I began my class with a surprise quiz. "Put your name on the top of the paper and number from one to ten." I asked my questions about the reading assignment and, as I did, glanced down at the paper of a student who sat right in the front. He was a great kid, and he would later go on to become a Ranger in the U.S. Army and a very successful adult. But when I collected the papers, he looked up somewhat sheepishly and asked, "Is this test going to count?" "Of course," I answered, although I knew it wouldn't affect his grade. What I understood from this interchange was that I could count on him doing every other reading assignment that I gave for homework.

Granted, not all students need as strong a lesson, and a similar tension could be created in gentler ways. In a Waldorf classroom, the times tables are always introduced with safety and support in mind. The children write down their times tables with colored pencils and recite them as a class rhythmically, beginning in first grade. The recitation is generally call and response and is often accompanied by rhythmic clapping and movement. However, at a certain age, if I didn't change my approach and create a charged atmosphere, learning for some students would progress too slowly.

This awareness was brought home by one of my sixth graders who had a quiet but noticeable aversion to math, and to the times tables in particular. From fourth grade to sixth grade, I would practice the six, seven, and eight times tables with the class continually. These are the hardest tables to memorize, and I didn't want my students to have trouble in the later grades with an algebra example like $(+6xy^2)$ $(-8x^3y^2)$ = and end up with $(-44x^4y^4)$, where the complicated work with signed numbers and exponents was done correctly but 6×8 was not. So, we practiced. I employed call and response recitation and rapid times table drills most mornings, and we did this together rhythmically and orally. However, what I noticed was that the student I mentioned was not saying her tables, but rather was just humming along. "Hmm = hmm, times, hmm." So I changed my place in the classroom and stood right next to her. She rolled her eyes at me unappreciatively, but started to speak: $54 = 9 \times 6$, $36 = 6 \times 6$, $48 = 8 \times 6$. My close proximity had removed her safety and her anonymity, both of which had been so appropriate in the early grades. By doing this repeatedly I helped her with her learning. (This student is now the parent of a Waldorf second grader, and as fate would have it, her daughter loves arithmetic.)

Too Soon

There are many remarkable lessons that Waldorf teachers have created. Some of these have been passed down by word of mouth from experienced colleagues, others are shared in teacher training programs and in publications. These lessons

In these diagrams the sequence of the times table's one's column is shown.

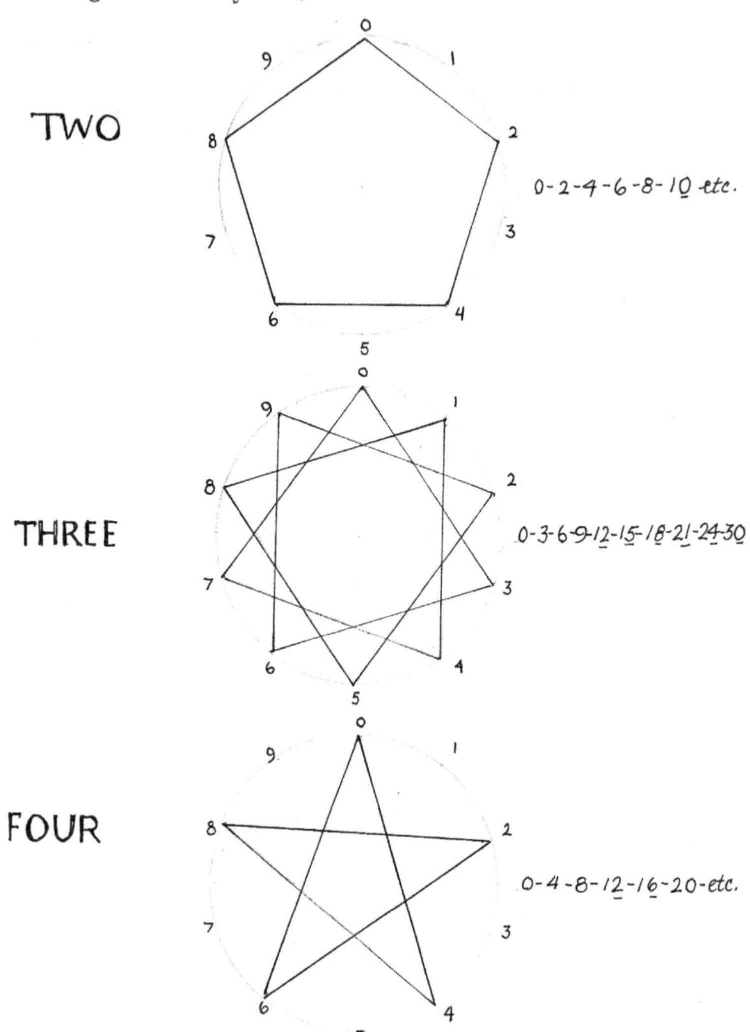

are treasures because they make it clear to both the teachers and the students that the world we live in is filled with wonder and meaning. The Chladni Plate, the Fibonacci Series, and the Golden Ratio are topics that can convey this wonder. There are also stories and legends that teachers get to tell that surprise and inspire, such as "The Gordian Knot," Michelangelo's carving of the *Pietà,* the first Marathon, and more. All of these help teachers to create lessons that make a dramatic impression on the students. Waldorf teachers are often aware of these topics and stories long before they occur in the curriculum. But if we teach them too soon or allude to them prematurely, we deprive them of their magic.

The first time I encountered this tendency in myself to introduce material prematurely was with the well-known and often-used times-table patterns. These patterns appear in Herman von Baravalle's little monograph, *The Teaching of Arithmetic in the Waldorf School Plan.*[*] These elaborate patterns occur with the two, three, and four times tables. I couldn't wait to share these with children and, unfortunately, I didn't. When I taught second grade for the first time, I created a template and led my students through the steps to produce these designs.

These forms were a revelation for me, but not for my second graders. They were too young. There was no "Wow!" I had simply brought this lesson too soon, and with teaching, timing matters.

With subsequent classes I introduced these patterns in third grade with much more participation on the part of the students. I also found other ways to deepen the experience. In our opening activities in arithmetic class, we could create

---

[*]   Baravalle, *The Teaching of Arithmetic and the Waldorf School Plan,* p. 14

these same stars by tossing a ball of yarn around the circle of ten students while we held on to one end of the yarn and sent it along reciting the numbers. We could also make the stars out of colored card stock with a needle and thread to give as gifts to their parents. I had learned from my mistake to curb my enthusiasm and to wait until the time was right. When you teach the same students for eight years, there is no reason to rush.

Too Late

It is, however, also possible to introduce subjects too late. Main-lesson blocks can often run longer than expected. When they do, they shorten the amount of time teachers have left to deliver the remainder of the curriculum.

I remember the end of the school year in my first fifth grade. I was passing our faculty chair in the hallway when he stopped and asked, "Jack, are you all right?"

I must have looked discouraged, but I was really just tired. In my early years of teaching, the written reports had to be completed and handed out on the last day of school. I had a large class, so I started my reports on May 1st, drafted one a day, and then rewrote them on Memorial Day weekend. No small feat.

I told Mr. Hoffmann that I was working on my reports and trying to complete the fifth-grade history curriculum. I had been preparing lessons on Sparta, Athens, Thermopylae, the Olympiad, and more. He looked at me closely and asked, "Why, is that your last block?" It was a good question. What I didn't mention in my reply was that I was struggling to complete the fifth-grade history curriculum. I knew I shouldn't teach ancient Greece in sixth grade as I had an older class and my students would be decidedly Roman. What I had needed was a better plan, one that would enable me to cover India, Persia, Babylon, Egypt, and Greek history, as well as Greek mythology, all in one year.

With my next class I made a conscious effort to meet this challenge and began the fifth grade by telling the Indian epic tale, *The Ramayana* (Elizabeth Seeger's version is excellent for telling) during our first arithmetic block. I wanted the children to hear this dramatic epic tale before we began our study of ancient India and Persia so it could serve as a foundation for the beginning of our history study. When we went on to study grammar later in the fall, we read a lovely shortened version of the Babylonian epic *Gilgamesh*. Then in the early winter we had a second history block devoted to ancient Egypt, to its remarkable art and culture with hieroglyphs, pyramids, and mummies. When we studied botany, I told the Greek myths that related to plants—Demeter, Narcissus, Hyacinthus, and Bacchus and Philemon. And when I introduced decimals, I told the *Odyssey*. This left ample time to make the transition from Greek mythology to Greek history, and of course the Olympiad. It took considerable focus and intention to teach the full history curriculum in fifth grade. With each of my following classes, it became easier. How I managed to do this was not as important as my resolve to deliver the full history curriculum in grade five.

The same issue occurred again in eighth grade with the modern history study. Ideally, an eighth-grade teacher's last history lesson should focus on the day's newspaper, because we are urged to have covered American and world history right up to the present day. However, eighth grade is an incredibly busy year with the eighth-grade play, the class trip, fundraising for the class trip, and more. Finding the time and the wherewithal to teach eighth grade history is a challenge. With my first class, we only got as far as the end of World War II. It seemed so unfortunate to end our history study without covering the Civil Rights Movement, the assassinations of John Kennedy and Martin Luther King Jr., the Vietnam War, Watergate, or the Iranian Hostage Crisis. And that was in 1981! There is now so much more history to cover since then. I was going to have to plan better and work harder and wait eight years to try again.

The demands of the upper grades' curriculum raise an important question that many schools are considering: Is it ideal to have the same class teacher go from grade one to grade eight?

Is One Class Teacher Enough?
Is One Class Teacher Not Enough?

I have often been asked, "What does it take to be a successful Waldorf class teacher?" My offhand response is usually "Schizophrenia." The truth is you have to be a very different teacher by the time you reach seventh and eighth grade than you were when you started out.

Imagine the first-grade teacher seated at the front of the room when a student approaches and sadly holds out a finger. The child says he has a cut, but there's no blood, not even a visible scratch because it's a paper cut. When this bothersome cut has been located, the teacher asks, "Would you like to have some cream put on it?" The child nods, for what he really needs is loving attention. The teacher then takes out a jar of cream and a cotton swab and proceeds to gently apply the sweet-smelling ointment to the paper cut and then the band aid. In the end this student is soothed and satisfied.

Now if a seventh grade student had a similar annoying cut and the teacher were to bestow that much attention— "up close and personal"—the middle school student would probably be repulsed. The adolescent can appreciate attention, but it generally shouldn't be so public and it shouldn't be overdone. The seventh and eighth graders value cool and respectful distance.

Many class teachers love working in the early grades because the connection with the children is obvious. The first graders follow the teacher everywhere. They take your hand unexpectedly, and they believe that sitting with the teacher at lunch is a treat. They even forget and call their teachers "Mommy" and "Daddy." But not all teachers are naturally suited for this. Some teachers feel smothered by this closeness and that their personal space has been invaded. In addition, having to create and maintain order in the midst of a series of endless needs—buttoning coats, removing boots, not to mention soothing hurt feelings—is more exhausting than they imagined when they were training to be teachers.

On the other hand, the teacher who is at home in the early grades can find that the middle school classroom feels like "enemy territory." The warm, caring, innocent children have been bewitched as they aged and have become unfriendly, loud, sometimes crude, and completely self-involved. A teacher could be left with the impression that if they were late to school or absent it could take the students twenty minutes to notice. But for the natural middle-school teacher this is all just fine. They appreciate their space and respect the student's need for theirs.

The question then arises: How do you start out with a core of needed attributes and over the course of six or seven years become a different person? That is the gradual, but noticeable path of personal and professional development for a class teacher.

On an inner level there are aspects of our soul nature that have to change. The tendencies we have through our character and our temperament need to be pruned, polished, and balanced. If we are quick to act, we need to shine the light of thinking on what we do. And if we have a thoughtful and observant nature, we need to make our participation more dynamic.

But there are also changes that need to occur on a professional level, because the middle-school curriculum is so much more demanding than the curriculum in the early grades. And coming to terms with the middle-school curriculum is crucial, because an effective and lively delivery of the curriculum influences the overall mood and discipline in the classroom.

When a class teacher specializes in teaching middle school, she or he is able to prepare the science and history blocks more frequently. This allows for a stronger understanding of the science demonstrations and the needed equipment. For history teaching, there can be a greater familiarity with biographies and a more comprehensive knowledge of certain historical periods. More frequent preparation enables teachers to modify their lessons and gather more resources. This is quite different from placing the quest for new material in an eight-year cocoon. The "specialized" middle-school teacher is able to stay up to date with the subjects, and this can result in a more effective teaching.

However, if a school decides to proceed with a different class teacher for grades six through eight, there are important questions to answer. The grade school is a time for developing good habits, and each Waldorf school must have a clear sense of which habits it wants to see nurtured in the preceding grades. Teachers who take over a class in sixth grade should legitimately expect that the students they receive will be good students.

During eighth grade many of the Waldorf students consider the possibility of going to another school for ninth grade. It happened one time that I asked a group of students who were in another class what kind of school they were looking for. They answered, "A good school." So I asked them, "What is a good school like?" Their answers were varied. Some said that a good school has good science labs, others said that a good school has a large gymnasium. Still others said that a good school has good teachers. I agreed with all of their comments, but said that there was something I thought they were missing. They were curious, so I told them, "Good schools have good students." I have always felt that it was a Waldorf school's assignment to help make the young people in its care into good students. Good students come to class on time. Good students listen attentively when a teacher presents and when a classmate speaks. Good students complete their assignments carefully and in a timely manner. In short, good students show up and are responsible. To instill these habits in the first five grades will take as much effort as delivering the curriculum in grades six, seven, and eight.

Considering the other perspective, what is the value of one teacher shepherding the students for all eight years? Is it the degree to which teachers know their students (and vice versa)? Is it the connection with the parents and the reassurance the parents experience when they have confidence that the teacher truly knows their child? Is it about the relationship between the teacher and the students? Was eight years with the same teacher what Rudolf Steiner originally had in mind? And last, is this still a workable model?

This is not a simple question, because each teaching situation is different. I had ample support with my last two eighth-grade classes, and it was never just my assignment. We had a team of teachers—English skills, math skills, eurythmy, handwork, woodwork, and a rich choral program (singing is so important in the middle school). In addition, with my last class I had a dedicated intern from our teacher training program who became my assistant. Her support enabled me to feel confident that my students were being held accountable.

If my school had decided to relieve me with a new teacher for middle school, I probably could have accepted that. But having been able to complete all eight years was a gift. If we take seriously what Rudolf Steiner said, then our striving and who we are as a teacher matters at least as much as what we teach.

One class teacher for all eight years can also work. If the example we provide for our students is that we are "learners" rather than simply "knowers," then we serve them, for learning continually is what they will need to do in life. If we offer them continuity in an era when families are so dispersed and neighborhood communities are continually in flux, we serve them as well. And if we demonstrate the value of seeing an assignment through to the end, we, like their parents, provide them with a model for how to approach significant undertakings in life.

It was deeply fulfilling to complete the eighth grade. We concluded the geography curriculum, which began in grade four with the most immediate surroundings, and then ended with a study of the entire world and a ten-minute sketch of the continents and oceans, which the students drew and labeled from memory. There was also an experience of deep satisfaction in completing the science curriculum, which began with the human being and the animal study in grade four and circled back to the human being in grade eight with anatomy and the meticulous drawings of the human skeleton. That same sense of completion was there with mathematics, as well, where the complicated algebra work reminded us of our first-grade studies of numbers and letters. We were closing the circle.

Yet, more than this, it was being with the students and watching them grow, seeing them mature, and listening to their discussions that was so deeply satisfying. I loved learning about the world with my students, for the world was what we studied during our eight years together. And I still miss being at the front of the classroom, greeting my students and asking them to stand to say the morning verse and feeling, just as Goldilocks did, "This is just right."

20

Wabi Sabi: The Beautifully Imperfect

The Japanese have an understanding we need in the west. They call it *Wabi Sabi*. It refers to moments that are beautifully imperfect, like a spring breeze blowing through the branches of a flowering cherry tree on a splendid day, causing the petals to fall, or objects like a cherished teacup with a chip, or a treasured but cracked ceramic bowl. What I came to realize was that as a teacher I needed to embrace this concept to help me better understand my work.

Years ago, I advised one of our twelfth graders on her senior project. The student was planning to do an illuminated text of the morning verse. She was an extremely capable student to whom I had taught calligraphy in sixth grade and in high school. After we talked over her project, we arranged for her to study gold-leaf lettering with an icon artist at a local seminary, after which she set to work with the rendering of the verse.

When she brought in her finished project, we looked at it together and it was beautifully done. The illuminated letter, the embellishments, the calligraphy, and the work in gold were all exceptional. Then we noticed the error. One word was misspelled—the "h" in the word *strength* was missing, and this student was crestfallen. She had no idea how to repair this project that had taken her weeks to complete, and neither did I. I tried to comfort her and mentioned that the

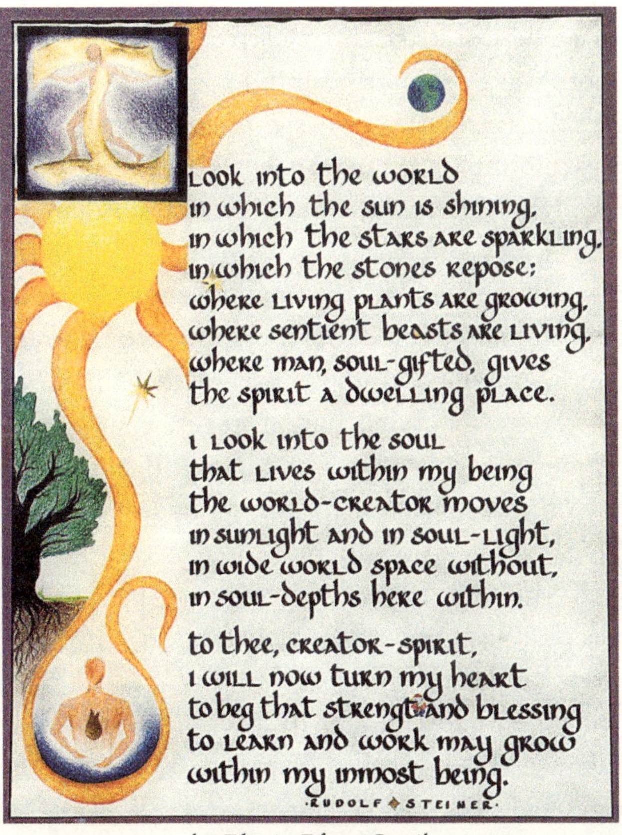

by Elenia Efron Guzik

medieval monks accepted their mistakes because the mistakes reminded them that only God is perfect and that to err is human. I also told her that in the Middle Ages the monks often drew a small, whimsical figure near a mistake to draw attention to the error. I asked Elenia to think about how she might repair her piece and I assured her that she would be able to solve this problem. When she came to school the next morning, she was glowing. "I figured it out," she said. And then she showed me her work. She had drawn a charming little gnome in colored pencil above the error. In its hands it held a gold-leaf letter "h" to correct the spelling omission. Her work was even more beautiful now.

Like the pearl inside an oyster or the gold-filled cracks in those extraordinary Japanese bowls, this student's work was exquisitely imperfect. Her senior project still hangs in our school hallway, and teachers have shown their students the gnome with the gold "h" to remind them that our mistakes are opportunities to make our work even more beautiful.

This is an important practice to develop in our students—the art of fixing our mistakes, a perfect twenty-first-century lesson, as our children will inherit a world filled with our mistakes. But this was also true with my teaching. Needless to say, there were numerous teaching moments and encounters with students, parents, and colleagues that were imperfect, moments when my shortcomings were unmistakably apparent.

There is a wonderful song by Peter Mayer that deserves a YouTube search.* It is called "Japanese Bowls," and hearing it always makes me feel better.

> I'm like one of those Japanese Bowls
> That were made long ago
> I have some cracks in me
> They have been filled with gold.
> That's what they used back then
> When they had a bowl to mend
> It did not hide the crack
> It made it shine instead.

I have always valued my failures. They have taught me so much more than my successes. Initially they showed me

---

* Mayer, https://www.youtube.com/watch?v=qOAzobTIGr8

where my teaching was thin on content and not sufficiently thought through. However, there were also times when I shifted the blame for the disappointing lessons away from myself and instead projected it onto my students. It was during those times when I would become annoyed and criticize a student. Even if that didn't happen outwardly, my mood could sour and the classroom atmosphere would be altered.

On the days when I was impatient, the regret would linger. It was on those days that I would feel a deep sense of disappointment in myself, and I would just think, "You don't want to be *that* teacher." It was this feeling of inadequacy and remorse that made it clear to me that I needed help.

Some of that help came in the form of self-help, my continuous effort to do better. Rudolf Steiner repeatedly pointed out that a teacher's inner struggle was more important than the perfect lesson. I believe that our heartfelt, honest striving creates a tangible spiritual substance for our students. So, when I regularly reviewed my teaching and found it wanting, I resolved to do better. I even went so far as to draw up a little calendar that I would look at every morning. I would make notes to myself on that calendar to help me remember what I needed to transform. For the first part of my teaching career, I believed completely in the importance of my inner work and striving, and that the improvement needed rested with me. But then I read the following statement by C. S. Lewis.

> When I come to my evening prayers and try to reckon up the sins of the day, nine times out of ten the most obvious one is some sin against charity; I have sulked or snapped or sneered or snubbed or stormed. And the excuse that immediately springs to mind is that the provocation was unexpected; I was caught off guard,

I had no time to collect myself.... Surely what a man does when he is taken off guard is the best evidence of the sort of man he is.... Surely, what pops out of a man before he has time to disguise it is the truth.

If there are rats in the cellar you are most likely to see them if you go in very suddenly. But the suddenness does not create the rats; it only prevents them from hiding. In the same way the suddenness of the provocation does not make an ill-tempered man; it only shows me what an ill-tempered man I am.... Now the cellar is out of reach of my conscious will.... I cannot by direct moral effort give myself new motives. After the first few steps, we realize that everything that needs to be done in our souls can be done only by God.*

When I read this statement, I realized that I believed this, too. I believed my inner striving mattered, and yet I also believed that "I had rats in my basement," and that without the help of the spiritual world I was destined to disappoint myself and my students. I was perplexed, because holding two seemingly opposite statements in my mind was unsettling. They seemed contradictory. It was only when I recognized the legitimacy of paradox that I came to terms with what I thought of at first as contradictory. I turned to Neils Bohr's understanding that "the opposite of profound truth can also be true."

I still embraced the need for my own inner work, but now I also recognized how essential it was to ask for help from the spiritual world. Prayer became a consistent part of my daily teaching practice. I know this sounds church-like, but Buddhists pray and so do Muslims, Jews, Native Americans, and the Maori and African peoples. Nearly the

---

*   Lewis, *Mere Christianity*, pp. 164, 165.

whole world prays, so I took up the notion, "Ask and you will receive," and found myself asking for help continually, asking for more patience, more tact, and more insight into children. This earnest asking, as much as anything, changed my teaching. My experience was that all of my requests were answered, especially when there was healing that was needed in a relationship with a student. In fact, by the end of my Waldorf teaching time, I was left wondering why I hadn't actively included the spiritual world in my teaching far more often. At a Waldorf school we believe that we don't teach alone, and yet I hadn't sufficiently walked the talk.

In looking back, I believe that my teaching career has been like one of those Japanese bowls. I have some cracks in me and yet, through my love of teaching, my commitment to my students, and my repeated resolve to do better, most of the cracks have been mended. At least I hope so. But it has only been through the ever-present help of the spiritual world that some of the cracks have been filled with gold.

Let me end by relating a dream that I had a number of years ago. My spiritual insights often come through dreams. Their meaning unfolds over time. Still, I have to apologize because the images in dreams can be so deeply personal and surprising. But the feeling that comes at the end of a dream is telling and is often more universal.

In the dream I was a journalist writing a piece about an elderly African-American man who lived in Washington, D.C. He worked in a city park, one with a park house, an extensive blacktop with playground equipment, and enclosed by a high cyclone fence. This man, dressed humbly in a tee shirt and overalls, walked with a limp and was viewed by the community as a living folk legend. His unique ability was that he was a remarkably skilled marksman with a bow and arrow. On the day I went to see him, he was going to demonstrate his skill.

As I watched, he walked to an old tree in the corner of the park and hung one of his bows on the trunk so that the bowstring was perfectly horizontal and the wooden portion of the bow curved below like a smile. Then he casually walked back a fair distance and with another bow he shot three arrows in quick succession. Each arrow landed just above the wooden bow inside the center of the smile. And each arrow was perfectly placed two inches above the previous one.

I turned to the man who had effortlessly accomplished this feat, and I asked him, "How did you do that?" He pointed to the high cyclone fence. Hanging on that fence was a large Christmas wreath and within the wreath a bright-white Russian Orthodox cross. "You see that?" he asked. "It is just a chakra, a symbol for the Living Spirit." Then he pointed behind me, and as I turned I saw an unusually tall panel of stained glass, one in which the colors pulsed dramatically. Just as I was about to wake, I was filled with sadness because I had never fully realized how imminent, alive, and vibrant the Living Spirit is. Its presence more than anything else has turned the lead of my teaching into gold.

Coda: A Foray into Public Schools

I knew this could work. For the last two years at Halloween, I had been invited by the librarian at a public school in northeast Washington, D.C., to tell stories to the children in the Day Treatment Center program. These were children who had been removed from their classrooms because of behavioral issues. They were in the early grades, first through fourth grade, and they were mostly boys, at least eighty percent. I was there to ask for their attention and to tell them a story. Each time I was there, they were better than good.

Just before I began to speak, one small, lively boy looked up at me and said, "You were here last year. You told that story about the mother who put a spell on a glass of milk and it turned as red as blood when her son was in danger." That was exactly what I had said, for I told "The Hairy Man," an African American folk tale that could possibly be the most engaging story for children to hear.

After my presentation was over, the boy's teacher came up to me and said how amazed she was that he remembered me and the story I had told the year before, because that child never remembers anything, and he can't sit still for more than ten minutes. But that day he sat quietly and listened for nearly thirty minutes.

I was pleased to hear the teacher's remarks but there was more on my mind. I had told stories to children for more than thirty years, and as a storyteller you can feel your audience's attention just as you can feel their restlessness when your tale wavers or when the story you're telling is not age appropriate. But you can also feel the moment when the children's attention is riveted. This generally occurs at a point of heightened tension. In the story I told that day, "Eagle Boy," a Native American story, the main character is faced with a significant decision: should he follow the clear and definite directions that he had been given by the Eagle, or give in to a strong impulse to do what he wanted to do? That was the moment when the children were completely spellbound.

Brain research shows that the part of the brain that is active when a story is heard is the same area of the brain that is active when a child is actually having that very experience. That is why stories are such an effective teaching tool. This was a significant moment for these children who knew first-hand the consequences of making the wrong choice.

In the 1990s in Marysville, California, Ruth Mikkelsen transformed a school for adolescent youth offenders into a Waldorf-based program for twelve to eighteen-year-olds who had been placed in her facility as part of their parole or as part of their sentence in lieu of time in a correctional facility. The program was remarkable. It effectively used the Waldorf curriculum for grades six, seven, and eight with the young people, and incorporated art, music, poetry, main lesson book work, and painting in their school experience.

I visited the school and had a chance to attend a main lesson and to see a watercolor painting class. I stood next to one of the older students at the end of the class as he showed his painting to the principal. "Is this good, teacher?" he asked, much the way a younger child would. His painting was extraordinarily beautiful, with vivid and intense colors as lovely as any that I had seen in Waldorf schools, and he deserved and received approval. As we left the room and entered the hallway, the principal turned to me and said, "You don't want to know why he's in here."

Waldorf education has much to offer mainstream education. That was the reason we started the Nova Institute. I had been speaking with a more experienced colleague who told me that he had recently attended a conference in California where more than a hundred and fifty independent schools were represented. Noticing their absence, he asked the organizers why the Waldorf schools were not there. He was told, "We invite them each year, but they're not interested."

It was clear to me that interest is a two-way street and until our Waldorf movement is interested in what goes on in other schools, we can't expect educators to pay much attention to our work. Perhaps this is part of the reason that we are often referred to as the "best kept secret" in education.

I also knew that our schools, and by that I mean our teachers, are busy, fully engaged with sustaining our schools and teaching the children. So, we started the Nova Institute to understand what other educators were doing, and to make common cause for the good of children everywhere. This wish took us into the city of Baltimore, where, in partnership with the Network for Enlivening Academics and the Safe and Sound organization, Laura Birdsall and I created The Enlivened Literacy Curriculum, which was designed to help the children in inner-city Baltimore improve their scores on the state MSPAP exam (Maryland State Performance Assessment Program), which had a sizable language and writing component.

The Enlivened Literacy experience led to a project in Washington, D.C., where I was hired to work extensively with children who had been removed from their regular classrooms and placed in a special Day Treatment Program. These children were the outcasts in the D.C. public schools. This undertaking was also a literacy program like the one in Baltimore whose evaluations had showed effectively improved vocabulary development, reading comprehension, writing fluency, and attendance. This new program would be for grades one through three and would also use storytelling, art, and drama to enhance the classroom learning experience for these students.

The initial objective of the program was student engagement. When children are engaged in a lesson—actively, emotionally, and thoughtfully—learning takes place. And what we knew from experience was that the storytelling would engage these children. It was our starting point. From there the students would be asked to draw their favorite part of the story, an activity that also successfully engages children, in particular, emotionally challenged boys who can focus themselves for a considerable amount of time with a drawing. Next the students would be asked to write a sentence or two about what they drew. When that routine was established after a week or so, it would provide the foundation upon which future learning could be built in other subjects.

I felt fortunate to be invited to begin this program in the very school where I had told my Halloween stories. I was excited. We ordered supplies—crayons, main lesson books, colored chalk, watercolor paints and paper, and colored pencils—and I began working on specific lessons.

But just two weeks before the program was set to begin, the arrangement fell through. At the end of August, the D.C. public system chose to move another school into the building to utilize unused space. Now my classroom was no longer available. All that could be offered as a replacement was the stage in the *all-purpose room,* a room used for lunch and gym classes. There was no way that highly active and easily distracted children could pay attention with so much going on around them. It was so disappointing, but the situation was no longer tenable.

The director of the program that had hired me began looking for another site. My only request was that I work with students in the early grades for whom our program was designed and specifically not with middle-school students. As it turned out, the only placement that was possible was a day treatment center for middle-school students just a few blocks from the U.S. Capitol. I was simply told, "Take it, or leave it." I was reluctant, but we had the supplies so I thought, "Why not?" That question would soon be answered.

When I showed up in my new classroom a week before school was set to begin, I found that I had been given a room with neither desks nor chairs, or even a blackboard. Trash was everywhere in the room, and at the front of the classroom there was an extremely large pile of old computer terminals, keyboards, discarded binders, and more. I was in disbelief. I began sorting and stacking the trash and placing it neatly in a corner at the front of my room figuring that the cleaning staff would take it away. I was wrong. The cleaning staff, I was told, was responsible only for the classrooms on the first and second floors in the regular public school. The program on the third floor for the challenged students, whom we were there to serve, was under a different division and not entitled to regular trash removal. So, I simply moved my pile (neatly) out to the hallway and worked on my classroom.

Next, I had to find desks and chairs. I was told to rummage through the other classrooms on our floor and see what I could find. Forget matching chairs and desks. I eventually found eight desks and a table and an assortment of chairs, some wooden, some metal, and some with imitation red leather upholstery, armrests, and buttons. I just needed one chair for each desk and two for the table.

Now I needed a blackboard. There was corkboard across one wall of the classroom and I decided to purchase a pint of blackboard paint and let that be my blackboard. After two coats of paint, my new classroom was ready.

The program for these older students would no longer focus on literacy and storytelling, but would now integrate arts-based instruction with the teaching of geometry. I began to plan geometric drawing lessons that would teach the students basic understandings, such as perpendicular lines, right angles, acute angles, bisecting arcs and angles, the various types of triangles, and more. But there was one more hitch. I was not permitted to give the students compasses with a point, as they had the potential to be used in class as weapons. I did some research and found that there actually are compasses without points and they were almost adequate for what we hoped to do. We were ready to begin.

I wanted to start with simple designs to help the students get accustomed to their new tools and to being able to follow sequential instructions. Each day new instructions were added and the learning was built on the previous day's experience. The only problem was that I had not anticipated the challenges of truancy. Students who were there for the first day's lesson didn't return for several days, and when they did it was as if they were starting over, while the students who attended regularly were making definite progress. The more serious unexpected absences were with the teachers. Homeroom teachers and subject teachers were also absent, particularly on Mondays, leaving the hall security staff to oversee the kids who were left unsupervised in the classrooms and roamed the halls. The sense of order at the school was fragile, to say the least.

When I came to school to teach my next class, I found that my colored chalk was missing from my desk and that the drawing that I had constructed on the blackboard had been partially colored in. I was told by the security staff which student had been in the room and decided to give him the opportunity to finish coloring in the drawing during class. It seemed like a good idea, but not to one of the girls in the class, who thought that this fellow did not deserve the privilege of drawing on the blackboard. She walked right up to the front of the room and, in no uncertain terms, told him that. The class froze as the two stood toe-to-toe as she was berating him.

I separated the two students. I asked L. (I'll never forget her real name) to take her seat, and I told the student at the board to get back to work. L. sat down, but she was still upset. She was one of the more creative students in the class, and I walked over to her desk and asked her to get back to work. She looked up at me and said, "I will if you f…ing help me!" I just gave her a look as if to say, "You expect me to help you when you speak to me like that?" It was clearly the wrong response, because L. stood up, took her chair, and threw it against the wall. She then turned to leave the room and took another chair and threw that one against the metal shelving on the other wall. On her way out she put her foot through the trash can that was by the back door. Right after she was gone, the student at the blackboard announced, "Well, Mr. Pee-trash, I guess she told you." I was shaken.

That day as I took the Metro train home from the school, I felt like a failure. I had been so hopeful about this opportunity to use the Waldorf approach to teaching with these students and it simply had not worked. As I exited my Metro stop, I was unexpectedly approached by a young man. Perhaps he saw the remains of my morning's experience on my face and in the way I walked, and he asked me how I was. I told him what had happened and how disheartened I was. What he said in reply helped considerably. "Remember, you can't reach all the children in those situations."

Shortly after this encounter our program ended because of concern for the safety of the teachers. Interviews were conducted with the students to assess their experience of the different classes that had been offered. By far the most positive responses were for the geometric drawing classes. The students missed the classes and they wanted to have the work they had done.

It has taken a number of years for me to process the experience of working in that Day Treatment Center. I still feel something in the pit of my stomach when I am in the neighborhood of that school. But I try to remember some of the successes. As I recall, it was often difficult to get the students to stop working at the end of our lesson and to move along to their next class. One quiet student in particular just kept working one day as I urged him to pack up and be finished. He looked up at me and said, "You know, you give me an ordinary pencil, I can't do much. But you give me colored pencils, I'm an artist."

I am convinced that all our students are artists, and I feel that the program we were offering was viable and valuable for a wide variety of reasons, not the least of which was allowing these under-served students an opportunity to be engaged in a creative and imaginative approach to learning.

ACKNOWLEDGMENTS

I was an unlikely candidate to be a Waldorf teacher. Seriously, I was a project and I would like to thank the individuals who have helped and supported me on my way.

Dr. Ron Schneebaum, my lifelong friend, who fifty years ago pointed me in the direction of a significant education course taught by Sheldon Stoff. Together, with Dr. Stoff's help, Ron and I met the work of Martin Buber, Franz Winkler, and Rudolf Steiner, and became Waldorf teachers.

John Gardner and Lee Lecraw for the life changing, formative experience of the Waldorf Institute in Garden City, New York, and for their invaluable guidance, which continued for years. I will always be indebted to both of these exemplary educators.

My friends and colleagues at the Washington Waldorf School, many of whom met me as a twenty-four-year-old kid from Queens, New York. They were both supportive and patient, but not called on to be nearly as patient as the many fine students that I taught there.

So many friends, colleagues, and future Waldorf teachers at the Rudolf Steiner Institute.

Trusted teaching friends—Bruce Libonn, Steven Levy, Jeff and Janet Kane, and Laura Birdsall—and my fine teaching companion Michele Coleman.

Anne Wotring, Bob Engelman, Greg Mueller, Carol Petrash and Jeri Darling—the board of the Nova

Institute—for twenty-one years of faithful participation and guidance.

Kathy Faltin and Ginny Smith, dear friends and extraordinary Waldorf teachers.

My sweet daughter, Ava, for her drawings.

Judy Blatchford and Ronald Koetzsch for their careful editing of my writing.

John Scott Legg at SteinerBooks for believing in this book and for all of his help and support in bringing it to print.

And lastly, to borrow a line from the writer, Ivan Doig, for my wife Carol, "Without you, darling, none of this would have been possible."

Bibliography

Baldwin Dancy, Rahima. *You Are Your Child's First Teacher: Encouraging Your Child's Natural Development from Birth to Age Six,* 3rd ed. Berkeley, CA: Ten Speed Press, 2012.

Baravalle, H. von. *The Teaching of Arithmetic and the Waldorf School Plan,* 3rd ed. Englewood, NJ: Waldorf School Monographs, 1967.

Benet, S. V. http://gutenberg.net.au/ebooks06/0602901h.html.

Bennis, W. G., and R. J. Thomas. *Geeks and Geezers: How Era, Values, and Defining Moments Shape Leaders.* Cambridge, MA: Harvard Business School, 2002.

Berry, W. *Collected Poems 1957–1982.* New York: North Point, 1987.

Brazelton, T., and S. Greenspan. *The Irreducible Needs of Childhood.* Cambridge, MA: Perseus, 2000.

Buber, M. *Between Man and Man.* London: Routledge and Keegan Paul, 1947.

Carter, S. *Dance in the Dark.* New York: Crossroad, 1982.

Coles, R. *The Spiritual Life of Children.* Boston: Houghton Mifflin, 1990.

Emerson, R. W. *Essays, First Series* ("Compensation"). New York: Penguin, 1977.

Falk, M. *The Book of Blessings: New Jewish Prayers for Daily Life, the Sabbath, and the New Moon Festivals* ("Will"). New York: Harper Collins, 1996.

Faraday, M. *The Chemical History of a Candle.* Glasgow: Good Press, 2019.

Ferguson, M. *The Aquarian Conspiracy: Personal and Social Transformation in Our Time.* New York: JPT Archer, 1987.

Flake, C. L. *Holistic Education: Principles, Perspectives, and Practices.* Brandon, VT: Holistic Education Press, 1993.

Friedman, T. *The World is Flat: A Brief History of the Twenty-first Century.* New York: Farrar, Straus, and Giroux, 2006.

Fullerson, M. C. *By a New and Living Way.* UK: Vincent Stuart, 1965.

Gardner, J. *Reflections on Discipline.* Great Barrington, MA: Myrin Institute, 1960.

———. *Right Action, Right Thinking.* Great Barrington, MA: Myrin Institute, 1969.

Giono, J. *The Man Who Planted Trees.* Chelsea, VT: Chelsea Green, 2007.

Gladwell, M. *Outliers: The Story of Success.* New York: Little Brown and Company, 2008.

Harrer, D. *Nature Studies for the Elementary Grades.* Garden City, NY: Waldorf Institute at Adelphi University, 1974.

Healy, J. M. *Endangered Minds: Why Children Don't Think—and What We Can Do about It.* New York: Touchstone, 1990.

Jacquet, H. *Christmas Plays from Oberufer: Paradise Play, Shepherds Play, Kings Play.* Forest Row, UK: Rudolf Steiner Press, 2007.

Johannson, F. "The Medici Effect." *The Urbanite* 33, Mar. 2007.

Kimmerer, R. W. *Braiding Sweetgrass: Indigenous Wisdom, Scientific Knowledge, and the Teaching of Plants.* Minneapolis: Milkweed Editions, 2013.

———. "Reclaiming the Honorable Harvest," TECx Talks. https://youtu.be/Lz1vgfZ3etE.

Kindlon, D. *Too Much of a Good Thing: Raising Children of Character in an Indulgent Age.* New York: Hyperion, 2001.

Knowles, Maria. "What's Lost as Handwriting Fades." *New York Times.* June 2, 2014.

Koepke, H. *Encountering the Self: Transformation and Destiny in the Ninth Year.* Great Barrington, MA: Anthroposophic Press, 1989.

Lewis, C. S. *Mere Christianity*. New York: Macmillan, 1952.

Lipson, M. *Stairway of Surprise: Six Steps to a Creative Life*. Great Barrington, MA: Anthroposophic Press, 2002.

Machado, A. *Selected Poems of Antonio Machado*. Middletown, CT: Wesleyan Press, 1983.

Mayer, Peter. "Japanese Bowls." Peter Mayer Music, 2010.

Mogel, W. *The Blessings of a Skinned Knee: Using Jewish Teachings to Raise Self-reliant Children*. New York: Penguin, 2001.

Muller, W. *Sabbath: Finding Rest, Renewal, and Delight in Our Busy Lives*. New York: Bantam, 2000.

Petrash, J. "Back to the Future." *Renewal*. Vol. 18, no. 1, 2009.

———. "How You Are Like Eagles." *Renewal*. Vol. 21, no. 2, 2012.

———. "Monday Morning Conspiracy." *Renewal*. Vol. 1, no. 2, 1992.

———. "The Third Grade: A Time of Transition." *Renewal*. Vol. 8, no. 1, 1999.

Pink, D. H. *A Whole New Mind: Why Right-Brainers Will Rule the Future*. New York: Riverhead, 2005.

Pipher, M. *The Shelter of Each Other: Rebuilding Our Families*. New York: Ballantine, 1996.

Ray, J. *Wild Card Quilt: The Ecology of Home*. Minneapolis: Milkweed Ed., 2003.

Rilke, R. M. *Letters to a Young Poet*. New York: Norton, 1993.

Robinson, K. "Creativity in Education," TED Talk. https://youtu.be /17Ye368aQVk.

Sanders, S. R. *Hunting for Hope: A Father's Journeys*. Boston: Beacon, 2000.

Schumacher, E. F. *Small is Beautiful: Economics as if People Mattered*. New York: Harper Collins, 1973.

Seton, E. T., and J. M. Seton. *The Gospel of the Redman*. Santa Fe: Seton Village, 1966.

Shore, B. *The Cathedral Within: Transforming Your Life by Giving Something Back.* New York: Random House, 2002.

Steiner, R. *Awakening to Community.* Spring Valley, NY: Anthroposophic Press, 1974.

——. *Balance in Teaching.* Great Barrington, MA: Anthroposophic Press, 2007.

——. *The Education of the Child: And Early Lectures on Education.* Hudson, NY: Anthroposophic Press, 1996.

——. *The Fall of the Spirits of Darkness.* London: Rudolf Steiner Press, 1993.

——. *The Foundations of Human Experience.* Great Barrington, MA: Anthroposophic Press, 1996.

——. *The Gospel of St. Luke.* London: Rudolf Steiner Press, 1964.

——. *How to Know Higher Worlds: A Modern Path of Initiation.* Hudson, NY: Anthroposophic Press, 1994.

——. *The Illustrated Buddha Path.* Boston, MA: Urban Press, 2000.

——. *Poetry and the Art of Speech.* London: London School of Speech Formation, 1981.

——. *Practical Advice to Teachers.* Hudson, NY: Anthroposophic Press, 2000.

——. *The Reappearance of Christ in the Etheric: A Collection of Lectures on the Second Coming of Christ.* Great Barrington, MA: SteinerBooks, 2003.

——. *Rudolf Steiner in the Waldorf School: Lectures and Addresses to Children, Parents, and Teachers.* Hudson, NY: Anthroposophic Press, 1996.

——. *Soul Economy: Body, Soul, and Spirit in Waldorf Education.* Great Barrington, MA: Anthroposophic Press, 2003.

MORRIS'S MANIFESTOS

ART, WEALTH AND RICHES

Art, Wealth
and Riches

WILLIAM MORRIS

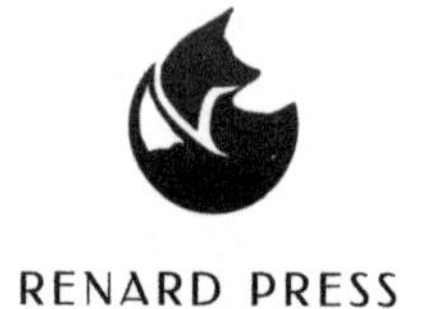

RENARD PRESS

RENARD PRESS LTD

124 City Road
London EC1V 2NX
United Kingdom
info@renardpress.com
020 8050 2928

www.renardpress.com

Art, Wealth and Riches first published in 1883
This edition first published by Renard Press Ltd in 2022

Edited text and Notes © Renard Press Ltd, 2022

Cover by Will Dady, after a design by William Morris

Printed on FSC-accredited papers in the UK by 4edge Limited

ISBN: 978-1-80447-026-8

13 12 11 10 9 8

CLIMATE POSITIVE Renard Press is proud to be a climate positive publisher, removing more carbon from the air than we emit and planting a small forest. For more information see renardpress.com/eco.

EU Authorised Representative: Easy Access System Europe
Mustamäe tee 50, 10621 Tallinn, Estonia
gpsr.requests@easproject.com

CONTENTS

ART, WEALTH AND RICHES

An address delivered at a joint conversazione of Manchester societies at the Royal Institution, Manchester, 6th March 1883*

RT, WEALTH AND RICHES are the words I have written at the head of this paper. Some of you may think that the two latter words, wealth and riches, are tautologous; but I cannot admit it. In truth there are no real synonyms in any language – I mean, unless in the case of words borrowed from another tongue – and in the early days of our own language no one would have thought of using the word rich as a synonym for wealthy. He would have understood a wealthy man to mean one who had plentiful livelihood, and a rich man one who had great dominion over his fellow men. Alexander the Rich, Canute the Rich,

Alfred the Rich;* these are familiar words enough in the early literature of the North; the adjective would scarcely be used except of a great king or chief, a man pre-eminent above other kings and chiefs. Now, without being a stickler for etymological accuracy, I must say that I think there are cases where modern languages have lost power by confusing two words into one meaning, and that this is one of them. I shall ask your leave, therefore, to use the words wealth and riches somewhat in the way in which our forefathers did, and to understand wealth as signifying the means of living a decent life, and riches the means for exercising dominion over other people. Thus understood the words are widely different to my mind; yet, indeed, if you say that the difference is but one of degree I must needs admit it; just so it is between the shepherd's dog and the wolf. Their respective views on the subject of mutton differ only in degree.

Anyhow, I think the following question is an important one: Which shall art belong to, wealth or riches? Whose servant shall she be? Or rather, Shall she be the slave of riches, or the friend and helpmate of wealth? Indeed, if I put the question in another form, and ask: Is art to be limited to a narrow class who only care for it in a very languid way, or is it to be the solace and pleasure of the whole people? The question finally comes to this: Are we to have art or the pretence of art? It is like enough that to many or even most of you the question will seem of no practical importance. To most people the present condition of art does seem in the main to be the only condition it could exist in among cultivated people, and they are (in a languid way, as I said) content with its present aims and tendencies. For myself, I am so discontented with the present conditions of art, and the matter seems to me so serious, that I am forced to try to make other people share my discontent,

and am this evening risking the committal of a breach of good manners by standing before you, grievance in hand, on an occasion like this, when everybody present, I feel sure, is full of goodwill both towards the arts and towards the public. My only excuse is my belief in the sincerity of your wish to know any serious views that can be taken of a matter so important. So I will say that the question I have asked, whether art is to be the helpmate of wealth or the slave of riches, is of great practical import, if indeed art is important to the human race, which I suppose no one here will gainsay.

Now I will ask those who think art is in a normal and healthy condition to explain the meaning of the enthusiasm (which I am glad to learn the people of Manchester share) shown of late years for the foundation and extension of museums, a great part of whose contents is but fragments of the household goods of past ages. Why do cultivated, sober, reasonable people, not lacking in a

due sense of the value of money, give large sums for scraps of figured cloth, pieces of roughly made pottery, worm-eaten carving, or battered metalwork, and treasure them up in expensive public buildings under the official guardianship of learned experts? Well, we all know that these things are supposed to teach us something; they are educational. The type of all our museums, that at South Kensington, is distinctly an educational establishment. Nor is what they are supposed to teach us mere dead history; these things are studied carefully and laboriously by men who intend making their living by the art of design. Ask any expert of any school of opinion as to art what he thinks of the desirability of those who are to make designs for the ornamental part of industrial art studying from these remains of past ages, and he will be certain to answer you that such study is indispensable to a designer. So you see, this is what it comes to. It is not to the

best works of our own time that a student is sent; no master or expert could honestly tell him that that would do him good, but to the mere wreckage of a bygone art, things which, when they were new, could be bought for the most part in every shop and marketplace. Well, need one ask what sort of a figure the wreckage of our ornamental art would cut in a museum of the twenty-fourth century? The plain truth is that people who have studied these matters know that these remnants of the past give tokens of an art which fashioned goods not only better than we do now, but different in kind, and better because they are different in kind, and were made in quite other ways than we make such things.

Before we ask why they were so much better, and why they differ in kind and not merely in degree of goodness, I want you to note specially once more that they were common wares, bought and sold in any market. I want you to note that, in spite of

the tyranny and violence of the days when they were fashioned, the beauty of which they formed a part surrounded all life; that then, at all events, art was the helpmate of wealth and not the slave of riches. True it is that then, as now, rich men spent great sums of money in ornament of all kinds, and no doubt the lower classes were wretchedly poor (as they are now); nevertheless, the art that rich men got differed only in abundance and splendour of material from what other people could compass. The thing to remember is that then everything which was made by man's hand was more or less beautiful.

Contrast that with the state of art at present, and then say if my unmannerly discontent is not somewhat justified. So far from everything that is made by man being beautiful, almost all ordinary wares that are made by civilised man are shabbily and pretentiously ugly; made so (it would almost seem) by perverse intent rather than by accident, when we consider how pleasant

and tempting to the inventive mind and the skilful hand are many of the processes of manufacture. Take for example the familiar art of glassmaking. I have been in a glass-house, and seen the workmen in the process of their work bring the molten glass into the most elegant and delicious forms. There were points of the manufacture when, if the vessel they were making had been taken straight to the annealing house, the result would have been something which would have rivalled the choicest pieces of Venetian glass; but that could not be – they had to take their callipers and moulds and reduce the fantastic elegance of the living metal to the due marketable ugliness and vulgarity of some shape, designed most likely by a man who did not in the least know or care how glass was made; and the experience is common enough in other arts. I repeat that all manufactured goods are now divided into two classes: one class vulgar and ugly, though often pretentious enough, with

work on it which it is a mockery to call ornamental, but which probably has some wretched remains of tradition still clinging to it – that is for poor people, for the uncultivated; the other class, made for some of the rich, intends to be beautiful, is carefully and elaborately designed, but usually fails of its intent, partly because it is cast loose from tradition, partly because there is no co-operation in it between the designer and the handicraftsman. Thus is our wealth injured, our wealth, the means of living a decent life, and no one is the gainer; for while on the one hand the lower classes have no real art of any kind about their houses, and have instead to put up with shabby and ghastly pretences of it which quite destroy their capacity for appreciating real art when they come across it in museums and picture galleries, so, on the other hand, not all the superfluous money of the rich can buy what they profess to want; the only real art they can have is that which

is made by unassisted individual genius, the laborious and painful work of men of rare attainments and special culture, who, cumbered as they are by unromantic life and hideous surroundings, do in spite of all manage now and then to break through the hindrances and produce noble works of art, which only a very few people even pretend to understand or be moved by. This art rich people can buy and possess sometimes, but necessarily there is little enough of it; and if there were tenfold what there is, I repeat it would not move the people one jot, for they are deadened to all art by the hideousness and squalor that surrounds them. Nor can I honestly say that the lack is wholly on their side, for the great artists I have been speaking of are what they are in virtue of their being men of very peculiar and especial gifts, and are mostly steeped in thoughts of history, wrapped up in contemplation of the beauty of past times. If they were not so constituted, I say, they would not in

the teeth of all the difficulties in their way be able to produce beauty at all. But note the result. Everyday life rejects and neglects them; they cannot choose but let it go its way, and wrap themselves up in dreams of Greece and Italy. The days of Pericles and the days of Dante are the days through which they move, and the England of our own day with its millions of eager struggling people neither helps nor is helped by them: yet it may be they bide their time of usefulness, and in days to come will not be forgotten. Let us hope so.

That, I say, is the condition of art amongst us. Lest you doubt it, or think I exaggerate, let me ask you to note how it fares with that art which is above all others co-operative: the art of architecture, to wit. Now, none know better than I do what a vast amount of talent and knowledge there is amongst the first-rate designers of buildings nowadays; and here and there all about the country one sees the buildings they have planned,

and is rejoiced by them. Yet little enough does that help us in these days when, if a man leaves England for a few years, he finds when he comes back half a county of bricks and mortar added to London. Can the greatest optimists say that the style of building in that half-county has improved meanwhile? Is it not true, on the contrary, that it goes on getting worse – if that be possible – the last house built being always the vulgarest and ugliest, till one is beginning now to think with regret of the days of Gower Street, and to look with some complacency on the queer little boxes of brown brick which stand with their trim gardens choked up amongst new squares and terraces in the suburbs of London? It is a matter of course that almost every new house shall be quite disgracefully and degradingly ugly, and if by chance we come across a new house that shows any signs of thoughtfulness in design and planning we are quite astonished, and want to know who

built it, who owns it, who designed it, and all about it from beginning to end; whereas when architecture was alive every house built was more or less beautiful. The phrase which called the styles of the Middle Ages Ecclesiastical Architecture has been long set aside by increased knowledge, and we know now that in that time cottage and cathedral were built in the same style and had the same kind of ornaments about them; size and, in some cases, material were the only differences between the humble and the majestic building. And it will not be till this sort of beauty is beginning to be once more in our towns that there will be a real school of architecture; till every little chandler's shop in our suburbs, every shed run up for mere convenience, is made without effort fit for its purpose and beautiful at one and the same time. Now just think what a contrast that makes with our present way of housing ourselves. It is not easy to imagine the beauty of a town all of whose houses

are beautiful, at least unless you have seen (say) Rouen or Oxford thirty years ago. But what a strange state art must be in when we either won't or can't take any trouble to make our houses fit for reasonable human beings to live in! Cannot, I suppose: for once again, except in the rarest cases, rich men's houses are no better than common ones. Excuse an example of this, I beg you. I have lately seen Bournemouth, the watering place south-west of the New Forest. It is a district (scarcely a town) of rich men's houses. There was every inducement there to make them decent, for the place, with its sandy hills and pine trees, gave really a remarkable site. It would not have taken so very much to have made it romantic. Well, there stand these rich men's houses among the pine trees and gardens, and not even the pine trees and gardens can make them tolerable. They are (you must pardon me the word) simply blackguardly, and while I speak they are going on building them by the mile.

And now why cannot we amend all this? Why cannot we have, for instance, simple and beautiful dwellings fit for cultivated, well-mannered men and women, and not for ignorant, purse-proud digesting machines? You may say, Because we don't wish for them, and that is true enough; but that only removes the question a step further, and we must ask: Why don't we care about art? Why has civilised society in all that relates to the beauty of man's handiwork degenerated from the time of the barbarous, superstitious, unpeaceful Middle Ages? That is indeed a serious question to ask, involving questions still more serious, and the mere mention of which you may resent if I should be forced to speak of them.

I said that the relics of past art which we are driven to study nowadays are of a work which was not merely better than what we do now, but differed in kind from it. Now this difference in kind explains our shortcomings so far, and leaves us only one more question

to ask: How shall we remedy the fault? For the kind of the handiwork of former times down to at least the time of the Renaissance was intelligent work, whereas ours is unintelligent work, or the work of slaves; surely this is enough to account for the worsening of art, for it means the disappearance of popular art from civilisation. Popular art – that is, the art which is made by the co-operation of many minds and hands, varying in kind and degree of talent, but all doing their part in due subordination to a great whole, without any one losing his individuality. The loss of such an art is surely great – nay, inestimable. But hitherto I have only been speaking of the lack of popular art being a grievous loss as a part of wealth; I have been considering the loss of the thing itself, the loss of the humanising influence which the daily sight of beautiful handiwork brings to bear upon people; but now, when we are considering the way in which that handiwork was done, and the

way in which it is done, the matter becomes more serious still. For I say unhesitatingly that the intelligent work which produced real art was pleasant to do, was human work, not over-burdensome or degrading; whereas the unintelligent work which produces sham art is irksome to do, it is unhuman work, burdensome and degrading; so that it is but right and proper that it should turn out nothing but ugly things. And the immediate cause of this degrading labour which oppresses so large a part of our people is the system of the organisation of labour, which is the chief instrument of the great power of modern Europe: competitive commerce. That system has quite changed the way of working in all matters that can be considered as art, and the change is a very much greater one than people know of or think of. In times past these handicrafts were done on a small, almost a domestic, scale by knots of workmen who mostly belonged to organised guilds, and were

taught their work soundly, however limited their education was in other respects. There was little division of labour among them; the grades between master and man were not many; a man knew his work from end to end, and felt responsible for every stage of its progress. Such work was necessarily slow to do and expensive to buy; neither was it always finished to the nail; but it was always intelligent work; there was a man's mind in it always, and abundant tokens of human hopes and fears, the sum of which makes life for all of us.

Now think of any kind of manufacture which you are conversant with, and note how differently it is done nowadays; almost certainly the workmen are collected in huge factories, in which labour is divided and subdivided, till a workman is perfectly helpless in his craft if he finds himself without those above to feed his work, those below to be fed by it. There is a regular hierarchy of masters over him – foreman,

manager, clerk and capitalist – every one of whom is more important than he who does the work. Not only is he not asked to put his individuality into his share of the work, but he is not allowed to. He is but part of a machine, and has but one unvarying set of tasks to do; and when he has once learned these, the more regularly and with the less thought he does them, the more valuable he is. The work turned out by this system is speedily done, and cheap to buy. No wonder, considering the marvellous perfection of the organisation of labour that turns it out, and the energy with which it is carried through. Also, it has a certain high finish, and what I should call shop-counter look, quite peculiar to the wares of this century; but it is of necessity utterly unintelligent, and has no sign of humanity on it; not even so much as to show weariness here and there, which would imply that one part of it was pleasanter to do than another. Whatever art or semblance of art is on it has been

doled out with due commercial care, and applied by a machine, human or otherwise, with exactly the same amount of interest in the doing it as went to the non-artistic parts of the work. Again I say that if such work were otherwise than ugly and despicable to look at one's sense of justice would be shocked; for the labour which went to the making of it was thankless and unpleasurable, little more than a mere oppression on the workman.

Must this sort of work last for ever? As long as it lasts the mass of the people can have no share in art; the only handicraftsmen who are free are the artists, as we call them today, and even they are hindered and oppressed by the oppression of their fellows. Yet I know that this machine-organised labour is necessary to competitive commerce; that is to say, to the present constitution of society; and probably most of you think that speculation on a root and branch change in that is mere idle dreaming. I cannot help it;

I can only say that that change must come, or at least be on the way, before art can be made to touch the mass of the people. To some that might seem an unimportant matter. One must charitably hope that such people are blind on the side of art, which I imagine is by no means an uncommon thing; and that blindness will entirely prevent them from understanding what I have been saying as to the pleasure which a good workman takes in his handiwork. But all those who know what art means will agree with me in asserting that pleasure is a necessary companion to the making of everything that can be called a work of art. To those, then, I appeal, and ask them to consider if it is fair and just that only a few among the millions of civilisation shall be partakers in a pleasure which is the surest and most constant of all pleasures, the unfailing solace of misfortune, happy and honourable work. Let us face the truth, and admit that a society which allows little

other human and undegrading pleasure to the greater part of its toilers save the pleasure that comes of rest after the torment of weary work – that such a society should not be stable if it is; that it is but natural that such a society should be honeycombed with corruption and sick with oft-repeated sordid crimes.

Anyhow, dream or not as we may about the chances of a better kind of life which shall include a fair share of art for most people, it is no dream, but a certainty that change is going on around us, though whitherward the change is leading us may be a matter of dispute. Most people, though, I suppose, will be inclined to think that everything tends to favour the fullest development of competitive commerce and the utmost perfection of the system of labour which it depends upon. I think that is likely enough, and that things will go on quicker and quicker till the last perfection of blind commercial war has been reached.

And then? May the change come with as little violence and suffering as may be!

It is the business of all of us to do our best to that end of preparing for change, and so softening the shock of it; to leave as little as possible that must be destroyed to be destroyed suddenly and by violence of some sort or other. And in no direction, it seems to me, can we do more useful work in forestalling destructive revolution than in being beforehand with it in trying to fill up the gap that separates class from class. Here is a point, surely, where competitive commerce has disappointed our hopes; she has been ready enough to attack the privilege of feudality, and successful enough in doing it, but in levelling the distinctions between upper and middle classes, between gentleman and commoner, she has stopped as if enough had been done: for, alas, most men will be glad enough to level down to themselves, and then hold their hands obstinately enough. But note what

stopping short here will do for us. It seems to me more than doubtful, if we go no further, whether we had better have gone as far; for the feudal and hierarchical system under which the old guild brethren whose work I have been praising lived, and which undoubtedly had something to do with the intelligence and single-heartedness of their work: this system, while it divided men rigorously into castes, did not actually busy itself to degrade them by forcing on them violent contrasts of cultivation and ignorance. The difference between lord and commoner, noble and burgher, was purely arbitrary; but how does it fare now with the distinction between class and class? Is it not the sad fact that the difference is no longer arbitrary but real? Down to a certain class, that of the educated gentleman, as he is called, there is indeed equality of manners and bearing, and if the commoners still choose to humble themselves and play the flunkey, that is their own affair; but below

that class there is, as it were, the stroke of a knife, and gentlemen and non-gentlemen divide the world.

Just think of the significance of one fact: that here in England in the nineteenth century, among all the shouts of progress that have been raised for many years, the greater number of people are doomed by the accident of their birth to misplace their aitches; that there are two languages talked in England: gentleman's English and workman's English. I do not care who gainsays it, I say that this is barbarous and dangerous; and it goes step by step with the lack of art which the same classes are forced into; it is a token, in short, of that vulgarity, to use a hateful word, which was not in existence before modern times and the blossoming of competitive commerce.

Nor, on the other hand, does modern class-division really fall much short of the caste system of the Middle Ages. It is pretty much as exclusive as that was. Excuse an

example: I was talking with a lady friend of mine the other day who was puzzled as to what to do with her growing son, and we discussed the possibility of his taking to one of the crafts – trades, as we call them now – say cabinetmaking. Now neither of us was much cumbered with social prejudices, both of us had a wholesome horror of increasing the army of London clerks, yet we were obliged to admit that unless a lad were of strong character and could take the step with his own eyes open and face the consequences on his own account, the thing could not be done; it would be making him either a sort of sloppy amateur or an involuntary martyr to principle. Well, really, after that, we do not seem to have quite cast off even the mere medieval superstition – founded, I take it, on the exclusiveness of Roman landlordism (for our Gothic forefathers were quite free from the twaddle) – that handiwork is a degrading occupation. At first sight the thing seems so

monstrous that one almost expects to wake up from a confused dream and find oneself in the reign of Henry the Eighth, with the whole paraphernalia in full blossom, from the divine right of kings downwards. Why in the name of patience should a carpenter be a worse gentleman than a lawyer? His craft is a much more useful one, much harder to learn, and at the very worst, even in these days, much pleasanter; and yet, you see, we gentlemen and ladies durst not set our sons to it unless we have found them to be enthusiasts or philosophers who can accept all consequences and despise the opinion of the world; in which case they will lie under the ban of that terrible adjective, eccentric.

Well, I have thought we might deduce part of this folly from a superstition of past ages, that it was partly a remnant of the accursed tyranny of ancient Rome; but there is another side to the question which puts a somewhat different face upon it. I bethink me that amongst other things the

lady said to me: 'You know, I wouldn't mind a lad being a cabinetmaker if he only made "Art" furniture.' Well, there you see! She naturally, as a matter of course, admitted what I have told you this evening is a fact – that even in a craft so intimately connected with fine art as cabinetmaking there could be two classes of goods: one the common one, quite without art; the other exceptional and having a sort of artificial art, so to say, tacked on to it. But furthermore, the thought that was in her mind went tolerably deep into the matter, and cleaves close to our subject; for in fact these crafts are so mechanical as they are now carried on that they don't exercise the intellectual part of a man; no, scarcely at all; and perhaps, after all, in these days, when privilege is on its deathbed, that has something to do with the low estimate that is made of them. You see, supposing a young man to enter the cabinetmaker's craft, for instance (one of the least mechanical, even at present); when

he had attained to more than average skill in it, his next ambition would be to better himself, as the phrase goes – that is, either to take to some other occupation thought more gentlemanly, or to become not a master cabinetmaker, but a capitalist employer of cabinetmakers. Thus the crafts lose their best men, because they have not in themselves due reward for excellence. Beyond a certain point you cannot go, and that point is not set high enough. Understand, by reward I don't mean only money wages, but social position, leisure and, above all, the self-respect which comes of our having the opportunity of doing remarkable and individual work, useful for one's fellows to possess, and pleasant for oneself to do; work which at least deserves thanks, whether it gets them or not. Now, mind you, I know well enough that it is the custom of people when they speak in public to talk largely of the dignity of labour and the esteem in which they hold the working

classes, and I suppose while they are speaking they believe what they say; but will their respect for the dignity of labour bear the test I have been speaking of? To wit, will they, can they, being of the upper or middle classes, put their sons to this kind of labour? Do they think that, so doing, they will give their children a good prospect in life? It does not take long to answer that question, and I repeat that I consider it a test question; therefore I say that the crafts are distinctly marked as forming part of a lower class, and that this stupidity is partly the remnant of the prejudices of the hierarchical society of the Middle Ages, but also is partly the result of the reckless pursuit of riches, which is the main aim of competitive commerce. Moreover, this is the worst part of the folly, for the mere superstition would of itself wear away, and not very slowly, either, before political and social progress; but the side of it which is fostered by competitive commerce is more enduring,

for there is reality about it. The crafts really are degraded, and the classes that form them are only kept sweet by the good blood and innate good sense of the workmen as men out of their working hours, and by their strong political tendencies, which are wittingly or unwittingly at war with competitive commerce, and may, I hope, be trusted slowly to overthrow it. Meanwhile, I believe this degradation of craftsmanship to be necessary to the perfection and progress of competitive commerce; the degradation of craftsmanship, or, in other words, the extinction of art. That is such a heavy accusation to bring against the system, that, crazy as you may think me, I am bound to declare myself in open rebellion against it – against, I admit it, the mightiest power which the world has ever seen. Mighty, indeed, yet mainly to destroy, and therefore I believe short-lived; since all things which are destructive bear their own destruction with them.

And now I want to get back before I finish to my first three words, Art, Wealth and Riches. I can conceive that many people would be like to say to me: You declare yourself in rebellion against the system which creates wealth for the world. It is just that which I deny; it is the destruction of wealth of which I accuse competitive commerce. I say that wealth, or the material means for living a decent life, is created in spite of that system, not because of it. To my mind real wealth is of two kinds: the first kind, food, raiment, shelter and the like; the second, matters of art and knowledge; that is, things good and necessary for the body, and things good and necessary for the mind. Many other things than these is competitive commerce busy about, some of them directly injurious to the life of man, some merely encumbrances to its honourable progress; meanwhile the first of these two kinds of real wealth she largely wastes, the second she largely destroys. She wastes the

first by unjust and ill-managed distribution of the power of acquiring wealth, which we call shortly money; by urging people to the reckless multiplication of their kind, and by gathering population into unmanageable aggregations to satisfy her ruthless greed, without the least thought of their welfare.

As for the second kind of wealth, mental wealth, in many ways she destroys it; but the two ways which most concern our subject tonight are these: first, the reckless destruction of the natural beauty of the earth, which compels the great mass of the population, in this country at least, to live amidst ugliness and squalor so revolting and disgusting that we could not bear it unless habit had made us used to it; that is to say, unless we were far advanced on the road towards losing some of the highest and happiest qualities which have been given to men. But the second way by which competitive commerce destroys our mental wealth is yet worse: it is by the turning of almost all handicraftsmen into

machines; that is to say, compelling them to work which is unintelligent and unhuman, a mere weariness to be borne for the greater part of the day; thus robbing men of the gain and victory which long ages of toil and thought have won from stern hard nature and necessity, man's pleasure and triumph in his daily work.

I tell you it is not wealth which our civilisation has created, but riches, with its necessary companion, poverty; for riches cannot exist without poverty, or in other words, slavery. All rich men must have someone to do their dirty work, from the collecting of their unjust rents to the sifting of their ash heaps. Under the dominion of riches we are masters and slaves, instead of fellow workmen, as we should be. If competitive commerce creates wealth, then should England surely be the wealthiest country in the world, as I suppose some people think it is, and as it is certainly the richest; but what shabbiness

is this rich country driven into? I belong, for instance, to a harmless little society whose object is to preserve for the public now living and to come the wealth which England still possesses in historical and beautiful buildings;* and I could give you a long and dismal list of buildings which England, with all her riches, has not been able to save from commercial greed in some form or another. 'It's a matter of money' is supposed to be an unanswerable argument in these cases, and indeed we generally find that if we answer it our answer is cast on the winds. Why, to this day in England (in England only, I believe, amongst civilised countries) there is no law to prevent a madman or an ignoramus from pulling down a house which he chooses to call his private property, though it may be one of the treasures of the land for art and history.

Or again, of how many acres of common land has riches robbed the country, even in this century? A treasure irreplaceable,

inestimable, in these days of teeming population. Yet where is the man who dares to propose a measure for the reinstatement of the public in its rights in this matter? How often, once more, have railway companies been allowed for the benefit of the few to rob the public of treasures of beauty that can never be replaced, owing to the cowardly and anarchical maxims which seem always to be favoured by those who should be our guardians herein; but riches has no bowels except for riches. Or you, of this part of the country, what have you done with Lancashire? It does not seem to be above ground. I think you must have been poor indeed to have been compelled to bury it. Were not the brown moors and the meadows, the clear streams and the sunny skies, wealth? Riches has made a strange home for you. Some of you, indeed, can sneak away from it sometimes to Wales, to Scotland, to Italy; some, but very few. I am sorry for you; and for myself, too, for

that matter, for down by the Thameside there we are getting rid of the earth as fast as we can also; most of Middlesex, most of Surrey, and huge cantles of Essex and Kent are buried mountains deep under fantastic folly or hideous squalor; and no one has the courage to say: 'Let us seek a remedy while any of our wealth in this kind is left us.'

Or, lastly, if all these things may seem light matters to some of you, grievously heavy as they really are, no one can think lightly of those terrible stories we have been hearing lately of the housing of poor people in London; indeed, and indeed no country which can bear to sit quiet under such grievances has any right to be called wealthy. Yet you know very well that it will be long indeed before any party or any Government will have the courage to face the subject, dangerous as they must needs know it is to shut their eyes to it.

And what is to amend these grievances? You must not press me too close on that

point. I believe I am in such a very small minority on these matters that it is enough for me if I find here and there someone who admits the grievances; for my business herein is to spread discontent. I do not think that this is an unimportant office; for, as discontent spreads, the yearning for bettering the state of things spreads with it, and the longing of many people, when it has grown deep and strong, melts away resistance to change in a sure, steady, unaccountable manner. Yet I will, with your leave, tell the chief things which I really want to see changed, in case I have not spoken plainly enough hitherto, and lest I should seem to have nothing to bid you to but destruction, the destruction of a system by some thought to have been made to last for ever. I want, then, all persons to be educated according to their capacity, not according to the amount of money which their parents happen to have. I want all persons to have manners and breeding according to

their innate goodness and kindness, and not according to the amount of money which their parents happen to have. As a consequence of these two things I want to be able to talk to any of my countrymen in his own tongue freely, and feeling sure that he will be able to understand my thoughts according to his innate capacity; and I also want to be able to sit at table with a person of any occupation without a feeling of awkwardness and constraint being pres-ent between us. I want no one to have any money except as due wages for work done; and, since I feel sure that those who do the most useful work will neither ask nor get the highest wages, I believe that this change will destroy that worship of a man for the sake of his money, which everybody admits is degrading, but which very few indeed can help sharing in. I want those who do the rough work of the world – sailors, miners, ploughmen and the like – to be treated with consideration and respect, to be paid

abundant money-wages, and to have plenty of leisure. I want modern science, which I believe to be capable of overcoming all material difficulties, to turn from such preposterous follies as the invention of anthracene colours and monster cannon to the invention of machines for performing such labour as is revolting and destructive of self-respect to the men who now have to do it by hand. I want handicraftsmen proper – that is, those who make wares – to be in such a position that they may be able to refuse to make foolish and useless wares, or to make the cheap and nasty wares which are the mainstay of competitive commerce, and are indeed slave-wares, made by and for slaves. And in order that the workmen may be in this position, I want division of labour restricted within reasonable limits, and men taught to think over their work and take pleasure in it. I also want the wasteful system of middlemen restricted, so that workmen may be brought

into contact with the public, who will thus learn something about their work, and so be able to give them due reward of praise for excellence.

Furthermore, I want the workmen to share the good fortunes of the business which they uphold, in due proportion to their skill and industry, as they must in any case share its bad fortunes. To which end it would be necessary that those who organise their labour should be paid no more than due wages for their work, and should be chosen for their skill and intelligence, and not because they happen to be the sons of moneybags. Also I want this, and, if men were living under the conditions I have just claimed for them, I should get it, that these islands which make the land we love should no longer be treated as here a cinder heap, and there a game preserve, but as the fair green garden of northern Europe, which no man on any pretence should be allowed to befoul or disfigure. Under all these

conditions I should certainly get the last want accomplished which I am now going to name. I want all the works of man's hand to be beautiful, rising in fair and honourable gradation from the simplest household goods to the stately public building, adorned with the handiwork of the greatest masters of expression which that real new birth and the dayspring of hope come back will bring forth for us.

These are the foundations of my Utopia, a city in which riches and poverty will have been conquered by wealth; and however crazy you may think my aspirations for it, one thing at least I am sure of, that henceforward it will be no use looking for popular art except in such an Utopia, or at least on the road thither; a road which, in my belief, leads to peace and civilisation, as the road away from it leads to discontent, corruption, tyranny and confusion. Yet it may be we are more nearly on the road to it than many people think; and however that

may be, I am cheered somewhat by thinking that the very small minority to which I belong is being helped by everyone who is of goodwill in social matters. Everyone who is pushing forward education helps us; for education, which seems such a small power to classes which have been used to some share of it for generations, when it reaches those who have grievances which they ought not to bear spreads deep discontent among them, and teaches them what to do to make their discontent fruitful. Everyone who is striving to extinguish poverty is helping us; for one of the greatest causes of the dearth of popular art and the oppression of joyless labour is the necessity that is imposed on modern civilisation for making miserable wares for miserable people, for the slaves of competitive commerce. All who assert public rights against private greed are helping us; every foil given to common-stealers, or railway philistines, or smoke-nuisance-breeders, is a victory

scored to us. Everyone who tries to keep alive traditions of art by gathering together relics of the art of bygone times, still more if he is so lucky as to be able to lead people by his own works to look through Manchester smoke and squalor to fair scenes of unspoiled nature or deeds of past history is helping us. Everyone who tries to bridge the gap between the classes, by helping the opening of museums and galleries and gardens and other pleasures which can be shared by all is helping us. Everyone who tries to stir up intelligence in their work in workmen, and more especially everyone who gives them hope in their work and a sense of self-respect and responsibility to the public in it, by such means as industrial partnerships and the like, is helping the cause most thoroughly.

These, and such as these, are our helpers, and give us a kind of hope that the time may come when our views and aspirations will no longer be considered rebellious,

and when competitive commerce will be lying in the same grave with chattel slavery, with serfdom, and with feudalism. Or rather, certainly the change will come, however long we shall have been dead by then; how, then, can we prevent its coming with violence and injustice that will breed other grievances in time, to be met by fresh discontent? Once again, how good it were to destroy all that must be destroyed gradually and with a good grace!

Here in England, we have a fair house full of many good things, but cumbered also with pestilential rubbish. What duty can be more pressing than to carry out the rubbish piecemeal and burn it outside, lest some day there be no way of getting rid of it but by burning it up inside with the goods and house and all?

NOTES

On the 6th of March 1883 William Morris gave a speech at the Manchester Royal Institution entitled *Art, Wealth and Riches*. It was first published in print form in *The Manchester Quarterly* in April 1883, and in *Architecture, Industry & Wealth: Collected Papers by William Morris* in 1902. Morris gave several versions of the speech on later dates, making so many changes throughout that the resulting speeches are generally considered to be variant essays. The text of this edition is based on that of the last printed edition, which is considered the authoritative text. For this edition spelling, punctuation and grammar have been silently corrected to make the text more appealing to the modern reader.

vii *Royal Institution, Manchester*: The Royal Manchester Institution was a learned society founded in 1823; it grew in scope,

and Manchester's first school of design opened in the building in 1838. In 1881 the Institution relocated premises to a building that is now part of Manchester Metropolitan University.

2   *Alexander the Rich, Canute the Rich, Alfred the Rich*: Morris demonstrates here the link between 'rich' and 'great' in replacing 'Great' in the names of Alexander the Great (356 BC–323 BC), Canute the Great (d. 1035), also known as Cnut, and Alfred the Great (849–99).

35   *I belong… historical and beautiful buildings*: This refers to the Society for the Protection of Ancient Buildings, which William Morris founded in 1877, along with his friend Philip Webb (1831–1915), British architect and designer.

A BRIEF BIOGRAPHICAL SKETCH OF WILLIAM MORRIS

William Morris was born on the 24th of March 1834 in Walthamstow to William, a financier in the City, and Emma, from a well-to-do Worcester family. The family lived in Woodford Hall, a mansion next to Epping Forest, and Morris spent much of his youth riding around Essex, marvelling at the architecture of the countryside churches. Sadly, his father died in 1847, and the distraught family were forced to move to smaller lodgings.

In 1852 Morris went to study classics at Exeter College, Oxford University, where he became associated with a group of artists that became known as the Birmingham Set.

Soon after leaving university he secured an apprenticeship with an Oxford architect, under the supervision of Philip Webb, and transferred to the London office, moving into

a Bloomsbury flat with fellow Birmingham Set member Edward Burne-Jones.

In October 1857 he met Jane Burden, and they married in April 1859, and moved to Great Ormond Street. Later that year Morris embarked on designing a house for the family, Red House, just outside Bexleyheath, and commissioned Webb to build it.

In 1861, along with partners Burne-Jones, Dante Gabriel Rossetti, Philip Webb, Ford Madox Brown, Charles Faulkner and Peter Paul Marshall, he founded the design company Morris, Marshall, Faulkner & Co., which they referred to as 'the Firm'.

From 1865 Morris's daily commute from Bexleyheath to central London began to take its toll, and he sold Red House and moved the family back to Bloomsbury, renting Kelmscott Manor in Oxfordshire with Rossetti as a country retreat from 1871.

In 1875 he assumed full control of the Firm, renaming it Morris & Co., and it went from strength to strength, meeting with particular

success with its textiles. He became increasingly politically active, founding the Society for the Protection of Ancient Buildings in 1877 and the Socialist League in 1884.

In 1891 he founded the Kelmscott Press, which focused on producing limited-edition illuminated books, making heavy use of his illustrations throughout, and involving the development of several typefaces.

It was around this time that his writing began to gain traction, and he met with success with his novels *News from Nowhere* (1890) and *The Well at the World's End* (1896). He also dedicated much time to translation, including several Icelandic sagas and a new rendering of Virgil's *Aeneid*.

Morris's final years were spent travelling in France and Norway, and holidaying in Folkestone at his doctor's suggestion, as a cure for his various ailments. He died of tuberculosis on the 4th of October 1896, leaving an indelible mark on the fields of design, literature and socialist thought.

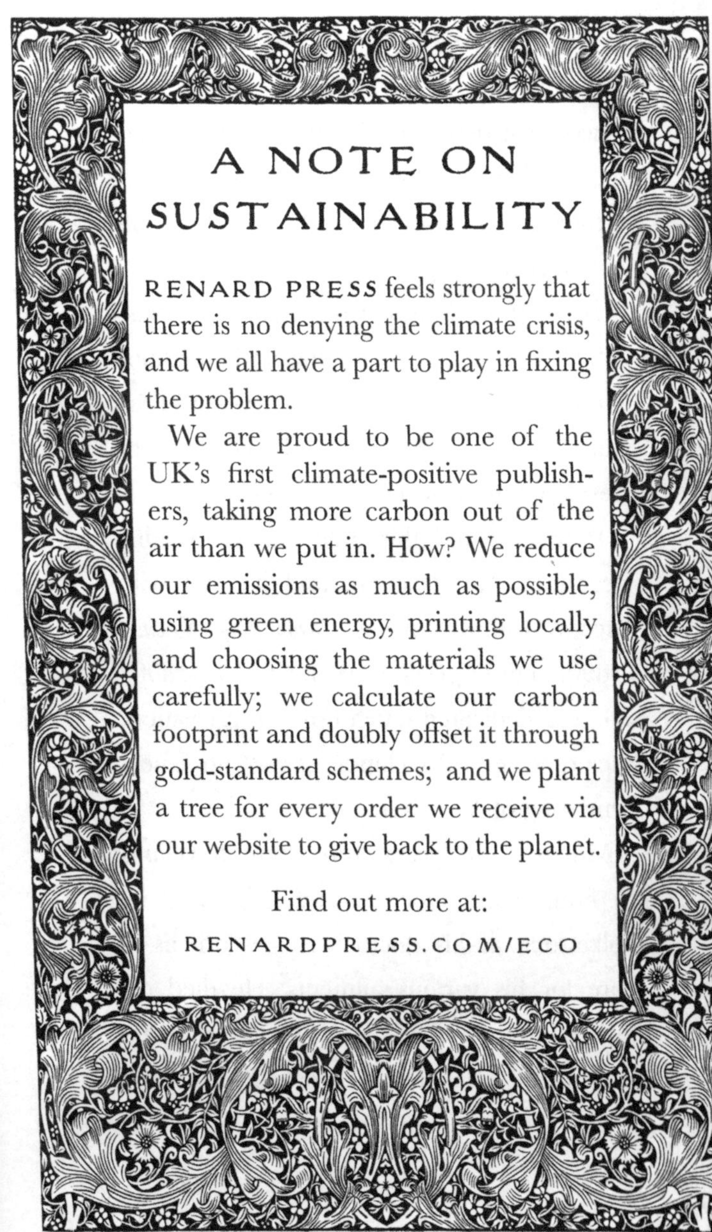
A NOTE ON
SUSTAINABILITY

RENARD PRESS feels strongly that
there is no denying the climate crisis,
and we all have a part to play in fixing
the problem.

We are proud to be one of the
UK's first climate-positive publish-
ers, taking more carbon out of the
air than we put in. How? We reduce
our emissions as much as possible,
using green energy, printing locally
and choosing the materials we use
carefully; we calculate our carbon
footprint and doubly offset it through
gold-standard schemes; and we plant
a tree for every order we receive via
our website to give back to the planet.

Find out more at:
RENARDPRESS.COM/ECO